GORDON THIESSEN

2407 West John Street
Grand Island, NE 68803
(308) 384-5762

HEADLINE SPORTS DEVOTIONS

Copyright © 1992 by Cross Training Publishing

Library of Congress Cataloging-in-Publication Data

Thiessen, Gordon D.

 Headline Sports Devotions / Gordon Thiessen

Published by Cross Training Publishing, Grand Island, Nebraska 68803

Distributed in the United States and Canada by Cross Training Publishing

Unless otherwise indicated, all Scripture quotations are from the *Holy Bible, New International Version,* © 1973, 1978, 1984, International Bible Society. Used by permission of Zondervan Bible Publishers. Other quotations are taken from *New American Standard Bible,* (NASB) © The Lockman Foundation 1960, 1962, 1963,1968, 1971,1972, 1973, 1975, 1977, the *Revised Standard Version of the Bible* (RSV) © 1946, 1952, 1971,1973, the *Authorized/King James Version* (KJV).

Cover Illustrator: Jeff Sharpton
Printed in the United States of America

Dedication

TO
The Grand Island Fellowship of Christian Athletes
Adult Chapter whose encouragement and friendship
I'll prize forever.

Acknowledgement

To my wife and children who have stood
by me and supported me, thank you!
Much appreciation to C.H. Hagstrom, Tim Leafblad,
and John Clinch for their comments and
suggestions on this book.
A special thanks to Jeff Sharpton for
his creativity on the cover design.

CONTENTS

INTRODUCTION

Jesus often taught by using parables and stories. He used settings and people that were familiar to his listeners. His stories related truth to the lives of those he taught.

Today, many of us relate to sports and the athletes who play them. While Jesus used parables and stories that related to his generation, my hope is that you will find the following sports headlines and devotions easy to relate to and apply to your life.

Headline Sports Devotions combines the issues and lessons taught in sports with a biblical perspective. Sports can teach us a lot of important lessons about life, but only when we understand it from God's perspective. Each devotion analyzes current sports headlines in light of Scripture. Hopefully, you'll find this dose of inspiration and perspiration helpful in your understanding of God's Word.

Everyone knows Bo. Most want to be like Mike. And a few even want to smell like Barkley. Millions watch sports and want to become like those they watch and read about. My goal for writing this book is for you to develop a desire to be like Christ, rather than Mike.

If you're reading through this book on your own, that's fine. I suggest you try to memorize each Scripture that is provided for each devotion. Also, ask yourself each of the Huddle questions. They'll challenge you to think through how the devotion applies to your life.

If you're reading through this book with a small group or a friend, be sure you discuss each of the questions. If you're the discussion leader, you might want to do some additional background preparation, since each of the devotions are designed for a brief discussion of the topic. You also might consider having different people take turns reading each of the devotions out loud. Following each headline in the table of contents, you"ll find a topic which relates to the headline. This will help you determine which devotion may be right for your group.

Headline Sports Devotions can also be used with a large group. It's easy to read it to the group—then break up into smaller groups for discussion.

For information on additional resources for Christian athletes and coaches write or call:

2407 West John Street
Grand Island, NE 68803
(308) 384-5762

Split Decision

Two polls and 119 voters—coaches, writers and broadcasters—couldn't settle on a single college football champion. College football's 1991 season ended Wednesday night with two different No. 1 teams—the Huskies in the USA TODAY/CNN coaches' poll, the Hurricanes in the Associated Press'—and that's the way it will stay. No playoff. No pickup game. And really, no complaints from either side. (USA TODAY)

A nice end to a great year of college football, isn't it? Well, at least if you're a Huskie or Hurricane fan it is. A split decision seems like the fair thing to do. And yet, wouldn't it have been great to see the two No. 1 teams play? But I won't complain. After all, I doubt if a split decision will cause either team to lose much sleep.

What seems fair in college football, doesn't work when it comes to following Christ.

Jesus said, "No one can serve two masters. Either he will hate the one and love the other, or he will be devoted to the one and despise the other. You cannot serve both God and money" (Matthew 6:24).

Jesus makes it clear; no split decisions when it comes to following heavenly or earthly values. It's not just tough to serve two masters, it's impossible. The word (masters) refers to a slave owner. You see, it's not like being employed and working for several people. It's the idea of giving full-time service and being totally controlled and obligated to one person. To give anything less makes the master less than a master.

We live in a society where a lot of people are materialistic and serve money. Jesus tells us: He's the Master. Not our credit card. Not the things we have. Again, it boils down to seeing things from His perspective. It's not easy when most advertising companies are trying to make us feel inadequate and discontent about ourselves. After all, they tell us, if we just buy their product it will solve all of our problems.

It's not just money that can become your master. It can be power, prestige, or trying to please other people. I repeat—anything, can push its way ahead of God on your priority list. Even sports can easily become your master. I've seen it happen many times. If you let athletics squeeze out the Lord for top priority—you're wrong.

You can't chase the world's dreams and honor God. Jesus said it, I didn't. So, you better make up your mind. Who's No. 1 in your life? If it's the world's values, it needs to change. One thing is for sure: God's not asking for your vote, He wants your life.

Huddle Discussion

• If your house were destroyed tonight, and you could choose to save three things, what would you pick?
• What occupies most of your thoughts, time and efforts?
• What will be valuable in heaven which isn't here?
• If Jesus were not your master, what would be?
• Which do you think is your master, money or God?
• If someone gave you $10,000, what would you spend it on?
• What does the Bible mean by "the love of money is a root of all kinds of evil?" (1 Timothy 6:10). Does this verse show you any trouble spots in your own life?
• How can you keep the Lord No. 1?

Just do it!

✔ Memorize: Psalm 16:8

Seaver storms into Hall of Fame

Three-time Cy Young Award winner Tom Seaver breezed into baseball's Hall of Fame Tuesday night with the speed of his awesome fastball, receiving the highest percentage of votes in the election's history. Pete Rose? He's still wondering what the Hall of Fame future holds for him. While Seaver was a shoo-in, Rose was a write-in. (USA TODAY)

What an honor for Tom Seaver. Not only to be elected into the Hall of Fame, but to get a record 98.8 percent of the votes. Can you imagine joining the likes of Hank Aaron, Babe Ruth, Mickey Mantle and Willie Mays?

Pete Rose would have been a lock to join Seaver in the Hall of Fame, had he not been banned from baseball.

In baseball, many will continue to argue in favor of Rose's being inducted into the Hall of Fame. But what about God's Hall of *Faith*? Is it different? Do we have to be perfect to get into it?

To get into the Hall of Fame it takes a certain type of athlete. For example, it may be somebody with a great fastball or tremendous speed.

But in God's Hall of *Faith* it doesn't require certain "type" persons. Any type will work. God didn't limit the exercise of faith to only ministers. Check out a list of different "types" in Hebrews chapter 11. It lists a farmer, businessman, homemaker, shepherd, King, songwriter, judge and a politician. Even the prostitute Rahab made the list.

Most Hall of Fame candidates have great records. Pete Rose has the record for all-time hits. Seaver had 331 victories, 3,640 strikeouts and one no-hitter.

Again, God's Hall of *Faith* is different. The inductees don't necessarily have a special record. And they're far from perfect. In fact, most of them had a weakness that God dealt with. For example: Moses murdered a man, Rahab was a prostitute, and Noah got drunk after the flood.

Aren't you glad that God's Hall of *Faith* isn't limited to a few spiritual giants? The people in Hebrews were like you and me. They believed God existed and trusted Him when faced with the tough circumstances.

The writer of Hebrews point is: faith is possible in anyone's life. Someday—maybe you'll storm into the Hall of *Faith*.

Huddle Discussion

• Who has been a person of great faith in your life? Why?
• Which of the faithful men and women of the Bible do you most relate to? Why?
• What does the Bible mean by "Now faith is being sure of what we hope for and certain of what we do not see" (Hebrews 11:1).
• How is your life different as a result of your faith in God?
• How does your faith affect others?
• Below are three areas that are affected by your faith or lack of faith. Discuss how your faith affects each one

    Attitudes • Trials • Occupation/School

• What goals can you set for each of the areas you discussed that are affected by your faith.
• Read Hebrews chapter 11. Which person do you most relate to in the chapter? Why?
(Check the cross-references in your Bible.)

Just do it!

✔ Memorize: Hebrews 11:1

SPORTS

Holdout slows Hornets' rookie

Two rookies made their professional debuts at Boston Garden Friday Night: No. 1 pick Larry Johnson, who signed a contract less than 48 hours earlier, and No. 24 pick Rich Fox, who signed the first weekend he was drafted. It wasn't hard to determine which player was more impressive. Fox scored 13 points in 21 minutes, and he bounded off the bench in the final quarter and made two huge defensive plays down the stretch. In short, he was a factor. Johnson was unable to stay on the floor because of poor conditioning. As a result, shortly after a brief offensive burst that helped Charlotte close within four in the final quarter, Johnson had to take a breather. The intent here is not to suggest Fox is a better player. The point is that by holding out until the 11th hour, Johnson is now forced to learn the NBA as he goes. (The Boston Globe)

If Johnson had been in the shape he should have been, Charlotte might have pulled off a big upset. Holdouts have become common in professional sports during the past decade. Every coach knows what results from a player who misses practice.

Johnson needed to take a breather every six minutes, because he was out of shape. What's true of physical conditioning is also true of spiritual conditioning.

To get into physical shape you need to run, jump, and practice. But to get into spiritual shape you need to pray, read the Bible, and meditate on God's Word.

The Apostle Paul said we are to train ourselves to be godly (1 Timothy 4:7). That's the goal of being spiritually fit. It's taking God seriously. When he speaks to us through the Bible, we listen and do whatever He asks.

So getting fit spiritually is a process. This process requires strict discipline and training. Larry Johnson didn't just wake up one morning physically fit to play in the NBA. Neither should you expect to get into shape spiritually, unless you spend time training yourself to be godly.

Paul also said "Everyone who competes in the games goes into strict training" (1 Corinthians 9:25). If an athlete trains himself to get a prize that is temporary, he said, how much more should we as Christians train ourselves to receive a crown that lasts forever.

In the NBA every team competes for the championship. Anything less—isn't good enough. No team wants to spend a lot of time training, only to go home a loser. But that's just what we sometimes do spiritually, isn't it?

It seems like a lot of us have forgotten that we are to run the race to receive the prize. Many of us run the spiritual race: unprepared, tired, and out-of-shape. We run the race as if we've forgotten about the prize.

Remember the prize and as the Nike commercial puts it— Just do it.

Huddle Discussion

• When have you been in your best physical shape? What was your training program?
• What kind of shape are you in *spiritually*?
Choose one of the following and discuss.
1) Iron Man   2) Marathon runner
3) Aerobic student   4) Got a 'C' in P.E. Class
5) Big but slow.
• What are doing to stay in shape spiritually?
• What could you change in your fitness program for godliness that would get you into better shape?
• What is the imperishable prize in 2 Timothy 4:8? Why should this motivate us to be spiritually fit?
• What can you do to get into spiritual shape? When will you plan to do it? How often?
• Read Hebrews 12:1. What do you need to do in order to run the race? What does it mean to throw off sin and hindrances?

Just do it!
✔ Memorize: 1 Corinthians 9:25

Marathoner, 54, reaches record 75 races in 1991

As Ed Barreto crossed the finish line in 5 hours and 32 minutes in the Upstate Marathon Sunday at Greenville, it was the end of much more than a 26.2-mile run. Barreto, 54, ran 75 marathons in 1991, breaking the one-year record of 74, set in April. "My knees are in bad shape. I'm all burned out," said Barreto. (USA TODAY)

Perseverance.

Now here is a guy who has it. I mean if anybody has it, this guy does. Perseverance has been defined as courage that is stretched out. And this is one runner who stretched it out, about as far as it will go.

Can you imagine what kind of physical stamina and mental toughness it must have taken for someone to run 75 marathons in a year? Not to mention the fact that he was 54 years old when he did it!

Determination.

That's another word that comes to mind when I think about what this 54-year-old accomplished. Determination is deciding to hang tough, regardless. You can bet that there were days when he must have wanted to call it quits.

Perseverance and determination are two important character qualities needed by every Christian. You see, the spiritual life of a Christian is much more like a cross-country run than a sprint.

I don't know how many times I've seen a young believer

in Christ start fast and fizzle-out before getting anywhere near the finish line. A marathon runner needs to develop the second wind, to make it over the long haul. He needs to develop the staying power to hang tough.

As a Christian, you don't need to gut it out on your own. It's a matter of relying on God for your strength. God can do amazing things through us, by His power. Jesus said, "... apart from me you can do nothing" (John 15:5). The Apostle Paul said, "Now to him who is able to do immeasurably more than all we ask or imagine, according to his power that is at work within us" (Eph. 3:20).

You have a choice. You can choose to gut out the spiritual race on your own and burn out. Or you can choose to depend on His power and finish the race with a kick.

Remember, when you are faced with an impossible situation, stretch out your courage, hang tough and depend on Him.

Huddle Discussion

• Have you ever experienced the "second wind" in sports? What did it feel like?
• When have you had to persevere?
• What was that time like?
• How did God strengthen you during this time?
• What did God teach you through this experience?
• Which characters in the Bible showed determination?
• Can we really do everything in Christ? "I can do everything through him who gives me strength" (Philippians 4:13).
• How can you remember to rely on God's power, rather than your weakness?
• How would you describe your relationship with God right now? 1) Nowhere 2) Up and down 3) In a holding pattern 4) Improving 5) Fantastic. How does your choice affect your perseverance and determination?

Just do it!

✔ Memorize: Philippians 4:13

AP Names Jordan Top Male Athlete

In leading the Chicago Bulls to the NBA crown last season and being named league and playoff MVP, Michael Jordan had the kind of year most athletes can only dream about. Several months earlier, Jordan replaced Soviet president Mikhail Gorbachev as the most admired male role model among high school students. (AP)

Is Michael Jordan a sports idol?

Does Jordan wear Nikes? You bet! You can also bet that Nike is banking on Michael continuing to be an idol to the sports world.

After all, are there any other athletes who have as much talent or personality? Maybe, but I sure haven't seen them. He sells shoes, videos, sports equipment, cereal, sports cards, magazines, gum, and just about anything else that they can put his picture on.

In the Bible, John warns us about idols:

"Dear children, keep yourselves from idols." (1 John 5:21)

Almost anything can qualify as an idol. You can make an idol out of anything or anyone. It might be your sport, a car, an award, a job, or even Michael Jordan.

Now, before you tear down your Michael Jordan poster, realize that there is nothing necessarily wrong with Jordan or any of the things I've listed. To possess any of these things is not wrong. But to let them possess us is wrong.

It would be nice and neat if I could give you a list of

things not to buy. It doesn't work that way. In fact, it's the good things I have the most trouble keeping in perspective. I've never really had to struggle with worshipping evil people or things. It's the good role models or things in life that more easily take the spotlight off God.

Jesus Christ needs to be the center of your life. It's easy to allow other things to take his place, but he wants to be first!

The Bible says, "And he is the head of the body, the church; he is the beginning and the firstborn from among the dead, so that in everything he might have the supremacy." (Colossians 1:18)

So what takes first place in your life? Is it your new car? How about your body? Anything—I repeat—anything that replaces God at the center of your life, is wrong!

Is God opposed to idols? Yes!

Does God care about being first in your life? You bet. C'mon, Christian, let's get our priorities straight. If there's one thing God will not tolerate, it's not being at the top of the list.

Huddle Discussion
• Who are your heroes?
• What makes each of these people a hero?
•Rank the following people and possessions based on how important they are to you. Then discuss your rankings.

____ Car
____ Clothes
____ TV
____ Music
____ Sports or cheerleading
____ Friends or dating relationships

• Are there any other things or people you would add to this list?
• Since Jesus is supposed to be first in your life, how should each of the items listed above be affected by this fact?

Just do it!
✔ Memorize: 1 John 5:21

Those shoes
Would you shell out $100 for a pair of Nikes?

It used to be that teen-agers saved their money to buy cars. Now they save up to buy athletic shoes. Yet—the pricey athletic shoe market seems to be on solid footing. Young shoppers know what they want, and most aren't willing to settle for less. Price is less of a consideration than style and color. They have to LOOK right. (Scripps Howard New Service)

Did you get that last statement? They have to LOOK right. One parent said, "We need to use some fiscal restraint, but we need to look at their need to feel good about the way they look, too."

I have to admit that I've bought shoes that cost more than $100. But I haven't yet shelled out that much for a pair of basketball shoes.

When I walk through the local sporting goods store—I'm amazed! There are shoes everywhere. All kinds of shoe colors, styles, and models cover the walls.

I grew up on "Chuck Taylor" black high-top tennis shoes. That's right tennis shoes. That's what all athletic shoes used to be called. I didn't necessarily pick them for performance— everybody had the same kind. Variety meant you wore low-tops, rather than high-tops.

Today, what you wear is a fashion statement. In fact, as I check out all the newest fashion statements, the clerk informs me that black is back. Good. Now I don't feel quite so old. Black shoes went from the only game in town to the last thing you'd be caught wearing. Black shoe sales are lacing up the top spot in the shoe market.

All this talk about shoes, and yet self-image is what it's all about, isn't it? How you LOOK is probably more important than saving a few extra bucks on shoes.

God has this to say about image: "So God created man in his own image, in the image of God he created him; male and female he created them" (Genesis 1:27).

This verse give us a solid basis for true self-worth. Worth that is not based on achievements, talent, or possessions. Instead, worth that is based on God's ability to make us into His image. Because you bear the image of God, you can feel good about yourself. After all, cutting down yourself is criticizing God for what He has made.

Isn't it great to know God gives each of us just the right LOOK. Best of all, Jesus shelled out the ultimate price for you and me. He died on a wooden cross to pay the price for your sin. Now, you just need to step into His shoes!

Huddle Discussion
• Which athletic shoes do you wear?
• What influenced you to buy this particular pair of shoes?
• What do the shoes say about who you are?
• Pick the top ten shoes on their LOOK.
• Would your ranking change if you ranked them on performance, rather than LOOK.
• Do looks matter to God? Rate each of the following on how much you think each matters to God.
(1) Matters a lot to God.   (2) Matters to God
(3) Matters very little to God.

      ____ My weight   ____ My clothes
      ____ My hairstyle ____ My grooming
• The Bible says you are "fearfully and wonderfully made" (Psalm 139:14). Is it hard for you to think of yourself like this?

Just do it!
✔ Memorize: Psalm 139:14

SPORTS

Streaky Rockets look for consistency

Don Chaney guided his Houston Rockets through rocky times last season when center Hakeem Olajuwon was out for 25 games with an eye injury. Chaney was named NBA coach of the year. He has his hands full again. The Rockets are grappling with backcourt shooting gone sour, an inconsistent offense and injuries. The Rockets have been the streakiest team in the NBA. "It's all about players concentrating and doing what they are capable of doing." Chaney said. (USA TODAY)

Nothing slows down a team like lack of consistency.

Coach Chaney's insight is to the point: "It's all about players concentrating and doing what they are capable of doing."

Every coach looks for consistency. If a team doesn't have it—they struggle. It's the glue that holds a team together over the long haul. Any team can put together a streak. Even the weakest of teams can win several games in a row. It's the great teams that practice and play consistently.

Four Superbowl rings for the 49er's. It didn't happen by chance. It happened because they were consistent for a decade.

God also looks for consistency. It's a mark of maturity.

Let's take a quiz. Keep your eyes on your own papers.

1. How often did you say something this week that you shouldn't have?
2. How often did you read your Bible this week?
3. Did you pray each day?
4. Did you show others that you loved and cared about

them?

5. Did you hang-out anywhere you shouldn't have?

Okay, how did you do? If you're like me, you probably feel at least a little bit guilty. It's not easy to be consistent, is it?

How do you become more consistent in your spiritual life? Spend time with God. It's really that simple—concentrate on Him and do what you are capable of doing.

Take time to develop habits that will help you be more consistent in your spiritual walk. It's true: "Sow a thought, reap an act; sow an act, reap a habit; sow a habit reap a character; sow a character, reap a destiny."

Timothy offers valuable advice on how to become more consistent in your spiritual life.

"All Scripture is God-breathed and is useful for teaching, rebuking, correction and training in righteousness, so that the man of God may be thoroughly equipped for every good work" (2 Timothy 3:16, 17).

Don't be a rookie in your spiritual life. Develop a consistent spiritual life by making it a habit to read and apply the Bible. Believe me, it's important to God. You can count on it.

Huddle Discussion

• Which athletic teams are the most consistent? What are two things about yourself that others can depend on?
• How would you compare your spiritual life to a football game? 1) Spectator 2) Bench warmer 3) Offensive player 4) Defensive player 5) Injured Reserve list
• In what spiritual areas are you a rookie or a veteran? Why?
• For you, what is the next step in your spiritual life?
1) Commit my life to Christ 2) Depend on Jesus for guidance each day 3) Work on basics—Bible study & prayer 4) Share my faith with friends and family 5) Reevaluate priorities

Just do it!
✔ Memorize: 2 Timothy 3:16, 17

Davis: Larkin to be scrutinized

Former Cincinnati outfielder Eric Davis, who was booed by Reds fans after signing a lucrative contract, expects Reds shortstop Barry Larkin to get the same treatment now that he has signed a $25.6 million contract. Davis says Larkin should be ready for higher fan expectations. "Once I signed a large contract, fans looked at me differently." Because of the higher expectations by the fans, Davis was booed whenever he struck out the past two seasons. (AP)

There is not much either Davis or Larkin can do about fan expectations. In fact, some might argue that it's part of being a pro athlete who makes millions of dollars.

The pressure to perform well, without failing, is not very healthy for those who live under someone else's expectations.

At all levels, fans demand high performance. It starts in Little League and never ends. It can consume those who watch and those who play.

Expectations have a way of bringing out the worst in us, rather than the best. It seems to depend on who sets the standard. When it's done, is it fair? Unbiased? Realistic? If it's not—expectations work against us, rather than for us.

What kind of expectations do you set for yourself? How about others? I'm sure most of us would just as soon have others leave us alone. Most of us of live in a fish bowl, even if we don't play sports.

While you can't do much about what others say and think, you can do something about the way you set expectations for others.

Give others a chance to be themselves. Don't make them into your own image. There are many personalities. Be thankful that God made you the way you are and the same for your friends.

The Bible says, "Accept one another, then, just as Christ accepted you, in order to bring praise to God" (Romans 15:7).

For Christians, this can be tough. Most churches are made up of people who only accept others based on what they did or did not do. This list of "do's and don'ts" or expectations is not biblical, but cultural. In other words, expectations might be based on how we dress, speak or look, rather than how we treat one another.

Let's pray that we can begin to accept others based on who they are in Christ, not on what they can do for us. Nothing is more frustrating than trying to live up to higher expectations than we can handle. Don't boo those who need love and acceptance. We already spend too much time scrutinizing one another and not enough time accepting each other.

The longer I live, the more I'm convinced that unrealistic expectations in the spiritual world lead only to frustration and stress, not to Christian maturity.

Huddle Discussion

• What do you think others expect of you in sports? Work? School? Home? Are these expectations realistic? Why?
• How do you feel when others put pressure on you?
• What "do's" and don'ts", which may or may not be biblical, frustrate you the most? Why?
• A common sin committed by many Christians is discrimination, racial or otherwise. The Bible calls this attitude—pride and conceit. (Romans 12:16). Is this a problem for your community? How can Christians be more accepting of other people?

Just do it!
✔ Memorize: Romans 15:7

Sun's Johnson realizes dream

Kevin Johnson's three-year dream to build a center for underprivileged youth became a reality Wednesday. "It didn't take a dream to realize that there were many youths who grew up with broken promises, said the Phoenix Suns guard in dedicating the 7,000-square-foot facility that will offer young people a home-like environment for study and recreation. "Someone needed to disrupt this vicious cycle," Johnson said. "I had a dream that on this lot, once a haven for drug users and transients, would be a place like this." (USA Today)

We don't read about many athletes who are following a dream like KJ's. The media seems to focus only on the athletes who are involved in drugs, rape, and cheating. Maybe media feeds us a steady diet of the negative stuff because it sells newspapers.

I don't know for sure. I do know that we need more dreamers like Kevin Johnson. People are hurting everywhere, but few of us are willing to reach out and help.

In the Christian community there are two extremes. One group pushes for knowledge at the expense of social action. The other group focuses almost entirely on social programs with little emphasis on Bible knowledge or sharing the gospel. Both extremes are wrong. In fact, I've learned that if Satan can't fool us with his lies, then he would like nothing better than to see us take the truth to extremes.

We need both evangelism (sharing the gospel) and social action. One without the other just doesn't work. I've heard it said, "People don't care how much you know until they know how much you care." I think that's true.

Jesus put it this way, "I tell you the truth, whatever you did for one of the least of these brothers of mine, you did for me." (Matt. 25:40)

This was a parable about the importance of caring for others. The point is we need to serve others where service is needed. He was teaching us to love and care for anyone who needs our help.

A lot of us might like the government to take care of the elderly or the homeless—but God made us responsible.

How about it? What can you dream of doing in your area? What difference can you make? Maybe it's time more of us became dreamers like Kevin Johnson, and showed people just how much we care...but be careful! Once you realize your dreams you'll never be the same. And neither will those you help.

Huddle Discussion
• Who are some people you've heard about who have reached out and showed compassion for others? What difference did they make?
• Do you remember a time when someone reached out to help you or your family? How did it make you feel?
• When have you reached out to others? How did it make you feel?
• Charles Colson, founder of the Prison Fellowship Ministry, has made a huge difference in the lives of inmates. Why do you think he has had so much success?
• Why don't more Christians spend time reaching out to those who need their help?
• What can you do in your community to help others? Make plans to serve someone else this week. Visit a hospital, collect cans for the food pantry, offer your help to a Salvation Army, etc. Pick something—then do it.
• Discuss James 2:15,-16 and 1 John 3:17.

Just do it!
✔ Memorize: Matthew 25:40

SPORTS

Deadeye Doyle a can't miss player

They call her "Deadeye Doyle." She has such a sure shooting touch, she hasn't missed a free throw in nearly a year. "I think I've been successful because I've been able to stay relaxed," says University of Richmond senior Ginny Doyle, who has extended her NCAA Division I women's basketball records for consecutive free throws to 59 (one season) and 65 (overall). (USA)

Now that's concentration. It must have taken tremendous concentration for her to set the free throw record.

God asks us to be deadeyes when it comes to meditating on His Word. Some think meditation just happens. Not true. Not anymore than becoming good at shooting free throws happens by daydreaming.

You see, meditation is not letting your mind wander all over the place. It's not chanting some meaningless phrase.

Let me explain what it is. Meditation is disciplined thought, focused on Scripture for a period of time. Do you get the idea? It's like reading a text to yourself. You quietly mouth the words over and over, trying to understand each word. It's the idea of whispering or muttering to yourself. So you talk to yourself about the passage, and also talk to God about it.

Mediation has been compared to how cows "chew the cud." In the morning milk cows eat grass for several hours like a lawn mower. Later in the morning, when they start to heat up, they lie under the shade tree and begin to cough up the little balls of grass that they have swallowed. Then they re-chew the cud until they know they have all the taste out of it. Finally, they swallow it into a second stomach compartment where it is digested and processed.

Meditation on God's Word is a similar type of digestion. When you think on His Word, your mind will be filled with His thoughts and ways.

The last step in meditation is application. This step asks the question, "What do I do now?"

Psalm 119 says, "Blessed are they whose ways are blameless, who walk according to the law of the Lord. Blessed are they who keep His statutes and seek Him with all their heart. They do nothing wrong; they walk in His ways. You have laid down precepts that are to be fully obeyed" (vv. 1-4).

Deadeye Doyle concentrates on each shot. Likewise, you need to concentrate on God's Word and ask yourself three questions:

What does it say?

What does it mean?

How does it apply to my life?

Ask these three questions and you'll be a can't miss Christian on God's team.

Huddle Discussion
• How has concentration helped you in your sport? Explain.
• How would you define meditation in your own words?
• What have you found to be a helpful way to understand what the Bible says? What do you do if you can't understand a part of the Bible?
• In what ways have you applied the Bible to your:
Sports? Relationships? Work? Other areas?
• Read Joshua 1:8 and Proverbs 6:22. What are some benefits from reading God's Word?
• Why would you tell someone that they should spend time reading and applying the Bible?

Just do it!
✔ Memorize: Psalm 119:1

Dream Team
Ten Picked for 1992 Olympic Team

We now know who is the greatest basketball team ever assembled. The first 10 members of the U.S. basketball team that will compete in Barcelona next summer were announced Saturday by USA Basketball.The players picked for the "Dream Team" included: Michael Jordan, Larry Bird, Magic Johnson, Charles Barkley, David Robinson, Patrick Ewing, Karl Malone, John Stockton, Scottie Pippen, and Chris Mullin. (AP)

Now here's a team I'd like to see play! And I'm sure they're eager to play. No arm twisting needed. To be chosen as part of this team is an honor.

In the past, U.S. national teams had been decided after a series of tryouts among invited players. Now that the pros are eligible that system has been scrapped, but not everyone is happy about the way players were picked.

In fact, there had been rumors that Isiah Thomas was being left off the team because of an ongoing feud between Jordan and him. Charles Barkley, rarely shy about speaking his mind, said this is nothing new. "Someone is going to be left off, it's all relative. Look at all the Olympic teams, someone has always been left off who people thought should have been on."

Yes, a team with the likes of Michael and Larry is a "Dream Team." How about the team that had the greatest impact on the entire world? That's right, you guessed it—the team Jesus chose, the disciples.

While the Olympic selection committee dug into every detail of a player's background and accomplishments so they could chose the right person, Jesus knew every detail of his team. Listen to what he said about one of his players: "I saw you while you were still under the fig tree before Philip called you." (John 1:48)

Jesus was talking to Nathanael, who was shocked that Jesus knew not only his name and where he had been, but also that he was an honest man.

Jesus' "Dream Team" is limited only by those he picks. And he picks those who follow him. Jesus knows every detail of your life. Eligibility is based on God's saving grace. Nothing else. No politics. Just the Master Coach, picking his team.

Just as Michael and Magic had to accept the invitation to play, so do you. God won't force you to be on his team, but he does want you to join. Here's your chance to be part of God's "Dream Team"—don't be left off!

Huddle Discussion

• Did you ever get left off a team when you were growing up? How did it make you feel?
• What was the best team you ever played on? What made the team good?
• Do you think most people believe that God has picked them to be on His team? Why?
• Why do most people think that they are part of God's team?
• Ephesians 2: 8,9 says, "For it is by grace you have been saved, through faith—and this not from yourselves, it is the gift of God—not by works, so that no one can boast." What does this verse say about how you become part of God's team? How is God's method different from how most teams are picked?

Just do it!

✔ Memorize: Ephesians 2: 8,9

HEADLINE SPORTS DEVOTIONS

Washington: Football capital

Everyone loves a winner. And today at noon, Washington salutes theirs—the Super Bowl Champion Redskins. The rally featuring the players and coaches, also will include city officials and a Washington staple, speeches. A large TV screen will make it easier for fans to see their heroes. The Redskins arrived home Monday afternoon to a cheering crowd of 1,500 at Redskins Park. In Buffalo, even with the 37-24 loss, Bills fans haven't cooled—approximately 10,000 gathered at City Hall to salute the team. (USA)

We love to praise the deeds of athletes, don't we? We praise them for what they have done and what they will do in the future.

Skins' fans went wild after their Super Bowl win—even the Bills' fans praised the efforts of their team. I have to agree with John Madden, "The largest gap in sports, is the gap between the winner and loser of the Super Bowl". Even though the Bills got ripped their fans responded with praise.

Praise is common in sports. We praise Jordan when he flies through the air and jams the basketball. We praise Barry Sanders when he dances and darts his way through opposing defenses.

Just as Redskin fans praise their team for what they have done: Likewise, Christians should praise God for all He has done for them.

If we can spend the time and energy to praise sports teams and heroes, why not God? He not only expects it, He demands it. Listen to what one writer in the Bible had to say about praise:

"Let everything that has breath praise the Lord. Praise the Lord". (Psalm 150:6)

What can you praise God for today? And not just the good things. After all, if 10,000 Bills' fans can praise their team when things don't go their way, can we do any less for God? It means praising Him when we're hurt, depressed, and confused. This is exactly the time we need to praise God more than ever.

Praise is both a response to God but also a step toward seeing God make changes in your life. You see, as you praise Him for what He has done and will do in your life, it frees you up to depend on Him. As you depend on Him, you become less dependent on yourself.

Did you praise God today? I hope you did, because as you praise Him, you'll begin to see just how much He loves and cares for you. Reebok tells us to "Pump it Up". I think it's time that Christians "Pump Him Up".

Just praise Him!

Huddle Discussion

• When did you go absolutely nuts cheering for a team or athlete?

• What made it so exciting?

• Do you think praising God is hard or easy? Why or why not?

• What two things happened recently that you can praise God for?

• When you praise God for what He has done for you, how do you feel? Why?

• In what ways can you praise God?

• You can praise God for His Word, character, and works. Make a list of things for each category.

Just do it!

✔ Memorize: Psalm 150:6

Like Gretzky, Hull model pro athlete

Unlike Wayne Gretzky, who has been giving more of himself than could be reasonably expected for nearly two decades, Brett Hull has only recently been in demand. But, like Gretzky, Hull chooses to treat people with decency and respect. Unusual? Sure it is. We live in an age where too many athletes use their massive egos and riches as excuses for acting like spoiled brats. Hull doesn't turn down requests for interviews or autographs.He doesn't maintain a scandalous lifestyle. (AP)

Is Brett Hull the perfect role model? Probably not. I'm not trying to be critical of him. In fact, by his own admission, he has said, "I find it hard to believe kids can look up to me that much."

I think a lot of athletes are puzzled by the admiration and respect they get. I haven't met anybody, yet, who hasn't had some sports hero or role model. Ask people between the ages of 35-50 about their favorite player, and you're likely to find out that it was Mickey Mantle. He was my hero, too. It doesn't seem like it was that long ago that I was collecting cards, magazines, gloves, baseballs—almost anything that had his name on it. Ask me about his statistics, and I can tell you all of his life-time figures for home runs and batting average.

Today the heroes or role models might be Michael Jordan, Barry Sanders, or Brett Hull. The faces have changed, but the relationships haven't. Kids and adults alike still love to watch and emulate their heroes.

A recent poll conducted by the Travelers Company showed that 37 percent of those polled selected athletes as the most positive role models. Pop artists got 14 percent and TV/movie stars got only 11 percent.

Every athlete, no matter how much we love them, will never measure up to our ultimate role model—Jesus Christ. Our sports heroes will continue to struggle with the same problems all of us do. If you get to know them, you'll see that they're really no different than the rest of us. Jesus is the one hero that will never let us down.

I doubt if Jesus shows up on most polls for positive role models—but he probably should. How can someone who lived 2,000 years ago be a positive role model? Hebrews 12:2 says, "Let us fix our eyes on Jesus, the author and perfecter of our faith… ." It's time we seek Jesus as our role model, and then let His light shine through us.

Huddle Discussion

• Which athletes have been your heroes? Name three and discuss each of your picks.
• Discuss which of the following you think make the best role models and why?
• Athletes • Rock star • Coach • Entertainer • Journalist
• Minister • TV or movie star • Parent • Politician
• What makes a person a bad or good role model? Read 3 John 11.
• Discuss each of the following statements?
"When kids ask me a question, I know whatever I tell them will be taken seriously." *Bruce Jenner (Olympic decathlon)*

"Role model? I don't care about role model! I just do what I have to do." Mike Tyson

"The larger the rock you drop in a quiet pool—the greater the ripples that radiate out from the splash…And the bigger the man—the greater his impact. Good or bad, it influences those around him. His sin moves out to cover the crowd—just as much as his righteousness." Dr. Richard Halverson

How can you make Jesus Christ your role model?

Just do it!

✔ Memorize: Hebrews 12:2

'Billion-in-one' homer
caps Braves comeback

Dave Justice hit a one-out, two-run homer off Rob Dibble in the ninth inning for a 7-6 victory over Cincinnati. Dibble had blown a game earlier in the season against the Braves, when he gave up a three-run homer in the ninth to set up a 10-9 win. What were the odds of rallying from a 6-0 deficit and then beating Dibble again on a ninth-inning homer? "About a billion to one," Justice said. "It's something you just don't do against the best relief pitcher in the game. You certainly don't do it twice," said another Brave. (AP)

What a comeback! Everyone loves to see a team beat the odds. Anybody who can beat the odds gets our attention. And why not? They've done something special and that makes them special.

Maybe, that's why there is so much interest in the predictions of sportswriters. They spend hours of their time researching and studying each team, so they can accurately predict the outcome of a game. The Bible also makes predictions.

Do you know what the odds are for someone fulfilling all of the prophecies that Jesus did? A prophecy is a prediction about some future event. Jesus fulfilled over 300 Old Testament prophecies.

Now, you might argue that some of them were coincidences. The chances of one man fulfilling just 8 of the major prophecies would be: one out of 10^{17}. That's more than 17 zeroes! Peter Stoner, using the modern science of probability, said, "That would be like taking 10^{17} silver dollars and lay them on the face of Texas. They will cover all of the state two feet deep. Now mark one of these silver dollars and stir the whole mass thoroughly, all over the state. Blindfold a man and tell him that he can travel as far as he wishes, but he must pick up one silver dollar and say that this is the right one."

Talk about a billion-to-one. In fact, if you take just 48 of those 300 prophecies the odds go up to 1 in 10^{157}.

You might be thinking, "Well, that sounds pretty impressive—but so what?" I don't know about you, but I figure that if Jesus made good on that many predictions—odds are, that he is who he said he was. After all, if Jesus fulfilled so many prophecies, then it only makes sense that he is who he claimed to be—the Son of God.

A 'billion-in-one' chance that Jesus would fulfill over 300 prophecies? You bet. You can also bet that Jesus was exactly who he said he was—the Son of God.

Huddle Discussion

• When did you play in a game where the outcome was a complete surprise?
• Why do you think God had Jesus fulfill more than 300 prophecies? What difference does it make to you that Jesus fulfilled so many prophecies?
• Jesus said, "Do not think that I came to abolish the Law or Prophets; I did not come to abolish, but to fulfill." (Matthew 5:17)
• What are some prophecies that you remember Jesus fulfilling? Which prophecy is the most important to you? Why?
• Look up the following scriptures on prophecy and their fulfillment: Isa. 7:14—Matthew 1:18, 24,25, Gen. 21:12—Luke 3:23,24, Micah 5:2—Matthew 2:1, Is. 40:3—Matthew 3:1,2, Ps. 16:10—Acts 2:31.

Just do it!
✔ Memorize: Matthew 5:17

'The Lord's Player' becoming more common in sports

During the 1970's the Baltimore Orioles employed a devout outfielder named Pat Kelly, who presided at clubhouse chapel services that seemed eccentric at the time but have since flourished. All that has changed. Today's managers are apt to stick little gold crosses in the crowns of their caps, and open prayer has overtaken sports. Where touchdown scorers used to boogie in the end zone, now they are more inclined to pray. (Washington Post)

Remember the Super Bowl a couple years ago, when several of the Giant's players prayed along the sidelines, as Buffalo attempted a last minute field goal? How about when Nebraska played Oklahoma in football in 1983? It was the first time I had ever seen players from both sides of the field start a game by praying together.

In many sports, the Christian faith has become more accepted in the locker room and on the field. Most pro teams have chapel programs before games. In fact, most college football programs have chapel services before their games. More players than ever are involved with Fellowship of Christian Athletes, Pro Athletes Outeach, Athletes in Action, and other sports-related ministries.

Sports Illustrated, among others, has questioned the appropriateness of prayer in the locker room or on the field. They wonder if prayer and play mix. Some think Christians have gone too far. While believers see opportunity, non-believers see red, or, in some cases, Bible verses written on huge banners draped over stadium stands.

What's the real issue? For Christians, it seems to be obedience. After all, God has told us to reach the world with the gospel (which includes sports fans).

Jesus said, "Go therefore and make disciples of all nations..." (Matthew 28:18). Jesus wasn't giving us an option—but a command to share our faith with others.

Maybe you're uncomfortable with sharing your faith with others. Maybe when you think of witnessing, you think of an evangelist. And you know you're anything but an evangelist. God gives each of us different gifts, but with the same responsibility. You may not be as outspoken or bold about your faith as Mike Singletary, and yet, God will give you opportunities to share, if you're faithful.

God doesn't necessarily ask you to lead thousands to Christ, though He might. He does command you to sincerely share what He has done in your life.

You know something? God may ask you to pray on a sideline, hang a sign at a game, or pray in the end zone. But don't count on it. More often than not, He just wants *you* to tell others how *He* has changed your life. Let's hope all of us make this more common in sports.

Huddle Discussion
• What are some examples of Christian athletes showing their faith in public? How did people respond?
• Do you think there are more Christians in sports today, than a few years ago? Why?
• Do play and prayer mix? Why or why not?
• Is it right for Christians to pray before, during, or after a competition?
• How aggressive should Christians be when they witness?
• In what ways should Christians witness?
• What is more important: To tell people about your faith or to live your faith out in front of them?

Just do it!
✔ Memorize: Matthew 5:16

Does faith lower batting averages?

Some conversations about a baseball players faith have resulted in headlines and debate. Such was the case when Gary Gaetti, hard-nosed leader of the Minnesota Twins' drive to a World Series title in 1987, became a "born-again" Christian the following year. Friction in the clubhouse developed. Gaetti's performance slipped. This season Darryl Strawberry is struggling to find balance between his faith and his game. On the Dodgers, Strawberry has lots of Christian supporters, among them Butler, Carter and Orel Hershiser, who hummed hymns in the dugout during the 1988 World Series and once said, "Just because I'm a Christian doesn't mean I'm a wimp." (USA Today)

Does faith lower batting averages? I doubt it. I'm not sure everyone agrees with me. In fact, *Sports Illustrated* asked this same question of Gary Gaetti, a couple of years ago, when he was in a hitting slump. And it seemed like every sports commentator thought that Darryl Strawberry's faith had affected his batting average—at least until he pulled out of his hitting slump toward the end of the year.

Can you be Christian and still be a hard-nosed competitor? Good question. Here are several athletes that believe you can be both.

"Anybody that says I would be docile about losing, I'd challenge him to stand in front of home plate with the ball and try to block me and see if I have lost my intensity to play." *Gary Gaetti-Angels*

"If Jesus were on the field, he'd be pitching inside and breaking up double plays. He'd be high-fiving the other guys. That's what Christianity is supposed to be. Some players may lose their fire, but not because of the Lord." *Tim Burke-Yankees*

"God doesn't want wimps. He doesn't want people who

are laid-back." *David Robinson-Spurs*

"You can be a Christian and still be a hard-nosed player. If Christ were a ballplayer, he'd be the best there was. He'd take out the guy at second base, then he'd say, 'I love you,' and pick him up, slap him on the butt and come back to the dugout." *Brett Butler-Dodgers*

Convinced? Well, don't take their word for it—take God's. God's Word says, "Whatever you do, work at it with all your heart, as working for the Lord, not for men." (Colossians 3:23)

Did you catch the word "whatever"? This verse applies to every sport. The word "heartily" refers to giving your best effort every time. No slacking off. No taking it easy. And the motivation? For the Lord, not for your coaches, teammates, or the fans.

Convinced yet? Maybe the real question is: Do you compete like your faith helps or hinders your athletics? I hope your faith helps. After all, if anything, your faith should raise your batting average, not lower it. God wants you to give your best…nothing more, nothing less, nothing else.

Huddle Discussion

• What does it mean to be a "competitive" athlete?
• Do you agree with the comments made by the athletes in this article? Why or why not?
• Do you think some athletes struggle with balancing their faith with sports? Why?
• If Jesus were on your team: What difference would it make? Describe how you think he would practice and compete.
• Is their ever a point at which a Christian athlete competes too hard? If so, when?
• Following a losing effort, a baseball player said, "It was God's will we lost". Do you agree with this type of attitude? Why or why not?

Just do it!

✔ Memorize: Colossians 3:23

The last shall be first Twins and Braves turn around last year's finish

No team in major league history had finished first in its division or league the season after finishing last. Then the Minnesota Twins and Atlanta Braves did in 1991. They went on to play in one of the most exciting World Series ever played. (The Sporting News)

It was an amazing turnaround. No one could have guessed that not just one, but two major league teams would go from last to first. To top it off, they played in one of the most exciting World Series ever.

No one team had ever come back from so far, let alone two teams! If this sports headline sounds familiar, it should. The Bible says pretty much the same thing in Mark 10:31, "But many who are first will be last, and the last first."

At first, this statement might sound confusing. But Jesus is clearly teaching that the values of this world will be reversed, in the world to come. The idea is that those who seek only status and importance here will lose out in heaven. Those who are humble here will be great in heaven.

In sports, as in our society, we are bombarded with messages that confuse our values. The world says we should seek fame and fortune. Jesus teaches that we should seek to serve others.

The rewards are different, too. While the Twins and Braves received their rewards here: status, money, and prestige. The rewards in God's kingdom are not based on earthly standards, but on a commitment to Jesus and following Him faithfully.

God doesn't call us to be successful—just faithful. That's not always an easy thing to keep in focus, in sports, where very little is said about faithfulness.

There are heavenly rewards that will be given out. Before you get excited about them, you'd better listen to what type of person will receive them.

First, those who are humble before God, who totally rely on Him, can count on a place in His kingdom.

Second, those who help the needy, those who are hurting, will receive much comfort in their own lives.

Third, those who are gentle—strong and yet with self control, will win out.

Fourth, those who are excited about righteousness, both heavenly and earthly, will receive from the Lord personal contentment and satisfaction.

If this list sounds familiar—it should. Each of these rewards and character traits are based on four of the eight Beatitudes found in the Bible.

God honors certain character traits and gives us particular rewards for each. Some of these rewards we'll see here and now—some we'll get later in heaven. One thing you can be sure of…God cares more about faithfulness to Him, than success that depends on this world.

Huddle Discussion

• Who did you want, the Twins or Braves, to win the 1991 World Series? Why?
• In what ways are the world's values confusing today?
• Read Matthew 5:1-12. How should each of these character qualities affect our lives?
• Are more people concerned with earthly rewards rather than heavenly rewards? Why or why not?

Just do it!
✔ Memorize: Mark 10:31

Collegians turn trash into art form

The first time Southern Cal point guard Duane Cooper took the court against Gary Payton, he received an education. Payton, then a star at Oregon State, now a pro, looked the 6-1 freshman over. "He walked up to me," said Cooper, "and said, 'I got a fresh one.' Then he nudged me real hard and tried to get the ref to call a foul." Michigan's "Fabulous Five" freshmen burst onto the college scene this season with their tongues honed almost as finely as their game. Welcome to the world of trash talk in college basketball. It has become an art—especially when a game is on national TV. (USA Today)

Talking trash is nothing new. It's been a part of sports for years, but it seems to be getting more media attention.

Most of the talk seems harmless. Like Shaquille O'Neal's remark to an opponent. He said, "I don't care how good you play, I'm still going to be the No. 1 draft pick." The other player's response was, "I thought about saying something back, but then I realized he was right."

The tongue is small but powerful. It's a lot like Barry Sanders. In the Bible, James refers to the tongue as a fire's spark.

Just as Barry Sanders is explosive, so is the tongue. If most of us are honest...we've probably talked a little trash ourselves. Please, no show of hands. Sports has a way of bringing out both the best and the worst in us. Listen to what the Bible says about the power of the tongue to influence and destroy:

"The tongue is a fire...a restless evil and full of deadly poison." (James 3:6,8)

No doubt about it—the tongue can do a lot of good or a

lot of damage. Does God really care if we take a shot at someone else?

Listen to what King David said in Psalm 39:1, "I will watch my ways and keep my tongue from sin; I will put a muzzle on my mouth."

Good advice. Another book in the Bible, Proverbs, is a good book to study if you want to know more about the power of our words. In fact, the terms tongue, lips, mouth, and words appear 150 times in this book about wisdom.

If anyone had a reason to talk trash it had to be Jesus. As Jesus was slandered, beaten, and crucified, he remained silent. He didn't lash out at those who had wronged him. He left the situation in God's hands. And so should we.

Tempted to let somebody have it? Caught in the grind of trash talk? Now's a good time to stop. Trust me, you'll never regret leaving the trash talk where it belongs.

Huddle Discussion

• When have you said something you wished you never said? When have you been hurt by what someone else said to you? How did it make you feel?

• Should Christians ever use foul language? When Christians do use it, what happens?

• Which of these actions are the worst? Rank each one and explain your reasons: ❑ Gossiping about a friend. ❑ Cussing out another player. ❑ Telling a dirty joke. ❑ Lying to a friend. ❑ Saying something that hurts your best friend. ❑ Boasting about something you've done.

• How can you keep from saying the wrong things?
Here are four ideas on how you can control the tongue:
1) Never say anything about someone unless you're willing to say it to their face. 2) Don't listen or respond to gossip.
3) Say positive things about others—not negative.

Just do it!

✔ Memorize: Psalm 39:1

Basketball born quietly in YMCA gym

Before Doctor J there was simply the doctor. He was James Naismith, a future M.D. who nailed up some peach baskets 100 years ago and invented Michael Jordan. Naismith's new game in the 1890s was decidedly earthbound—to the point that when infrequent baskets were scored, ladders were used to retrieve the ball. Not until 1913 were the bottoms taken out of the baskets. (USA Today)

I doubt if Dr. Naismith could ever have dreamed that his game would change so much during the past hundred years. Julius "Dr. J" Erving sent it into orbit in the 1970s, and Michael Jordan carries it heavenward in the 1990s.

Could he ever have dreamed that Nike would build a shoe empire on Jordan's ability to fly? Or that basketball players would make millions of dollars each year to play a kids' game?

While I'm impressed that a game born quietly in a YMCA gym would become a billion dollar industry, I'm more impressed by the quiet birth of a Jewish carpenter 2,000 years ago.

You know, Jesus Christ. We celebrate his birth each Christmas. Although the importance of it often gets lost in the busy-ness of the season. The Bible says, "The Word became flesh and made his dwelling among us." (John 1:14)

God entered this world as a baby. He was born in a quiet stable, that no doubt smelled from the animals. The floor would have been hard and dirty.

Could anyone have dreamed that the God of the universe would make such a quiet and lowly entry into the world? I'm sure a lot of people never knew the Savior of the world was born that night. Not because they were doing bad things, but because they weren't looking. Some things haven't changed in two thousand years.

How about you? Are you looking for the Savior? Do you understand how the world has been quietly changed by a little baby born two thousand years ago?

Have you noticed how his birth has forever changed the course of history? Do you understand the significance of the most important event in history? The Master Inventor provided mankind with a way to salvation—Jesus Christ.

Are you too busy to notice the most important event in your life and mine? Maybe it's time you looked beyond the creation and to the Creator. Don't forget to thank God for inventing a way to save us from ourselves.

Huddle Discussion

• If you could chose one sports event in history to attend, which one would you chose? Why?
• What was the most important news event the year you were born? (If you don't know how about the decade?)
• What changes took place when Jesus came to earth?
• How is history different because of the birth of Christ?
• Why are some people too busy to notice Jesus Christ?
• How does your family celebrate the birth of Jesus?
• The birth of Christ is called the *incarnation*. According to *Unger's Bible Dictionary*, it means, "that gracious, voluntary act of the Son of God in assuming a human body and human nature." How does this definition help you understand what God has done for us?

Just do it!

✔ Memorize: John 1:14

Friday the 13th!
Major League players share superstitions

Ozzie Guillen won't wash his clothes. Erik Hanson won't step on the white lines. Duane Ward won't play catch with anyone except Jim Acker. Ball players, beware. It's Friday the 13th. Call them crazy, kooky or flat out weird. Whatever, when it comes to good-luck charms or home-style hexes, look out. There are major superstitions in the minors, too. Take Wendell Turk. Occasionally, he pitches without socks. Or he'll chew licorice and brush his teeth in the dugout. Or he'll draw three crosses in the dirt on the back of the mound, then lick the dirt off his fingers." (AP)

Where's Freddie Krueger when you need him? Talk about ridiculous! Other ball players chew certain gum, eat a particular food, or spit their chew in the same place every game. The number of superstitions among baseball players alone could fill a book.

How about you? Do you have a few superstitions? I have to confess, I wore my midget football jersey all the way into high school. Not over my pads you understand, but under them. It was my lucky charm. It was number 66, and I bought it because my football hero wore the same number. I thought, just maybe, some of his skill, talent, luck, or whatever might just rub-off on me.

It's an interesting thing about that old torn-up jersey. When I played college football my freshman year, it mysteriously disappeared. I still suspect someone in my family. However, one of my teammates might have been sick of seeing and smelling the thing. You know what? I didn't play any differently without it. I can't say I was really surprised. After all, I didn't really believe it helped. Or did I?

More often than not, our little superstitions become stumbling blocks to us. Rules that somehow we've made up or believe affect the way we live.

The same thing can happen in our spiritual lives. It's easy to let man-made rules replace God-made guidelines for living the Christian life.

Remember the time Jesus healed the man by the pool in John chapter 5. The man had been an invalid for 38 years. Jesus healed him, but the religious leaders were upset because their picky laws forbid it.

What kind of man-made rules or superstitions do you believe about the Christian faith? Does length of hair or dress make someone less spiritual? Do you play and compete better simply because you pray? Do you use prayer like a rabbits foot?

Superstition does one thing—it binds you. It enslaves you to a set of rules that makes life miserable. Especially when you create man-made rules for living your faith. Break the chains of superstitions and man-made rules. Never forget that Jesus Christ can liberate you. "Then you will know the truth, and the truth will set you free." (John 8:32)

Huddle Discussion

• What kind of superstitions did you believe when you were younger?
• Do you still have some habits or superstitions that you follow today? If so, what are they?
• Have you heard of any other superstitions of athletes? What are they?
• What kind of man-made rules or superstitions do other Christians believe?
• Why do Christians set up rules and regulations that are not based on God's Word? How do they affect us? Others?
• If you could change one man-made rule, what would it be?

Just do it!
✔ Memorize: John 8:32

Glory and Gloom

As Bonnie Blair won more gold, Dan Jansen endured more disappointment. It is the nature of speed skating that the difference in the Olympic fortunes of Bonnie Blair and Dan Jansen amounted to a couple of hundreths of a second—maybe the width of a skate or the wavelength of a vibe, good or bad. Blair's skates glided smoothly, but something seemed to drag at Jansen's. The result was that while Blair had added gold to gold, Jansen only added disappointment to tragedy. (Sports Illustrated)

It was Bonnie Blair's third gold medal in the Olympics. For Dan Jansen, who was the world-record holder at 500 meters, it was bitter disappointment. You probably remember his story. Four years ago he learned of his sister's death just before he raced in the 500 and 1,000 meter sprint. In both, he not only failed to win, but he also slipped and fell on the ice.

It's hard to imagine the disappointment that Olympic athletes feel when they fail. After all, they train for four years for a competition, which may last only seconds. Then to lose by a fraction of a second or to win against the world's best must bring to surface a lot of emotions.

It reminds me of the lead into ABC TV's Wide World of Sports. Remember? "The thrill of victory, the agony of defeat." First you see several athletes celebrate their victories. Then you see the poor skier crash and burn. It kind of sums up the emotions every athlete feels after competition, even if only for a brief moment.

How do you deal with disappointments? As I watched the other athletes compete during the Olympics, I noticed that some got angry, others cried, and a few were emotionless when they lost. Can you lose and not be upset or disappointed?

The book of James helps us understand how to respond to disappointment. "Consider it pure joy, my brothers, whenever you face trails of many kinds, because you know that the testing of your faith develops endurance" (James 1:2).

It's important to understand two things about troubles from this verse. First, disappointments are inevitable. It's true in sports, isn't it? You just can't win every time you compete. Second, disappointment has purpose. The testing of our faith produces endurance. So God is teaching us endurance and helping us grow in our faith.

The point is not to pretend to be happy about our disappointments but to have a positive attitude about them. The Bible teaches that there is a difference between joy and happiness. Happiness is a feeling, but joy is an attitude.

You see, happiness depends on circumstances, but joy is always a choice we can make. We can't avoid pain and disappointment, but we can choose joy over misery.

The next time you lose or are disappointed by something; remember, God is helping you grow in your faith and gives you the option of choosing joy over misery.

Huddle Discussion

• If you could be in the Winter Olympics, which event would you chose? Why?
• What was your most disappointing loss or performance? How did you feel after it?
• Do you think Christian athletes handle disappointment better than non-Christians? Why or why not? Can you think of any examples?
• Describe how your attitude toward disappointment can affect you and others? How about future competition?
• What helps you deal with disappointment?

Just do it!
✔ Memorize: James 1:2

Daring, nerves and guts: The life of a speedskier

Someone compared a speed skiers descent down the first third of the slope, built at a 76-degree angle, to falling off a cliff. They fell down the slope in a tuck position, a vapor trail of snow behind them. As they passed the timing area, a faint rumble was audible more than 50 feet away, like a jet passing in the distance. The effect of watching them pass, one colorful blur after another, was numbing, like standing on the tarmac at a major airport, watching planes land. (Dallas Morning News)

That's a pretty good description of what speed skiing looks like. Not that I've actually had the chance to see it for myself, aside from TV. Watching the 1992 Winter Olympics on TV, gave me a new level of respect for the speedskiers.

It does take daring, nerves and guts to be a speedskier, doesn't it? It's dangerous—as we saw when one of the skiers lost his life to an accident, while practicing for a race in the 1992 Winter Olympics. A speedskier reaches speeds of more than 130 mph on the slippery slopes. I can't begin to imagine the fear and pain they must feel when they fall. It must be almost like jumping out of a moving car and tumbling totally out of control.

The life of a Christian can require just as much daring, nerves and guts. In fact, it takes all three of these qualities to resist negative peer pressure. Listen to the warning God gives in 1 Corinthians 15:33, "Do not be deceived, 'Bad company corrupts good morals,'" (v.33) *The Living Bible* puts it this way, "Don't be fooled by those who say such things. If you listen to them you will start acting like them."

In other words, if we spend enough time around the wrong people, our actions become like theirs. That's really common sense, isn't it? We would all like to think that we would be a greater influence on the people we're around, than they would be on us. But often, their actions rub off more on us, don't they?

It takes daring, nerves and guts to think for yourself, resist the crowd influence, and take a stand for Jesus Christ. Don't forget, you're never really alone. After all, God said he would never leave or forsake you. So my advice is:

Don't let others pressure you to do things in order to be accepted by them. Instead, speak up for your own beliefs and follow God's standards in the Bible.

Huddle Discussion

• What two sports do you think take the most daring, nerves and guts? Why?
• In what ways is peer pressure like "monkey see, monkey do"?
• When someone is trying to get you to do something you believe is questionable or wrong, what is the best way to say no?
• How would you suggest someone can stand tall for Christ?
• Give your advice for each of the following situations:

a. When your best friends are around the wrong crowd, it's easy for them to talk them into doing wrong things.

b. Jill is uncomfortable when she dresses differently than the rest of her friends.

c. Bob never takes a stand for Christ at school. In fact, most of his friends would be shocked if they knew he were a Christian.

d. Monica has trouble going to parties and saying no to either alcohol or drugs that are sometimes available.

Just do it!
✔ Memorize: 1 Corinthians 15:33

Ceballos dunks blindfolded

Cedric Ceballos already had the Slam Dunk Contest won Saturday when he masked himself with a black blindfold and raced three-quarters the length of the floor and jammed the ball home. The first time Ceballos tried what he calls his hocus-pocus dunk, last Christmas, he missed the basket completely. But after working out with Sun's gorilla mascot, Ceballos improved to 40% accuracy. "I couldn't see at all," Ceballos said of Saturday's dunk. "I marked off 20 steps, but when you're running, it counts down to 10." (USA Today)

Wow! Now that's NBA magic. Well… at least if he really couldn't see from behind the blindfold. There was a minor dispute following his dunk regarding the blindfold. Although he didn't allow the officials to inspect it, he was able to convince them that he couldn't see with it on.

When I think of Ceballos' feat, I can't help but think of all the times Jesus talked about spiritual blindness. In fact, the New Testament is full of references about spiritual blindness. Jesus often used something everyone understood, like blindness, to make a point about the spiritual life.

When the disciples told Jesus that the religious leaders were offended by some of the things he said, Jesus responded by saying, "Leave them, they are blind guides. If a blind man leads a blind man, both will fall into a pit" (Matthew 15:14).

Jesus was making it clear to the disciples that they needed to leave the religious leaders alone. Just ignore them. They were blind to the truth. Anyone who listened to them, risked spiritual blindness.

Today there are a lot of religious leaders who claim to

have a lock on truth, but lack spiritual eyesight. I'm not necessarily talking about the pastor at your church. I have in mind all the cults that have sprung up in America during the past decade. It's great to live in a country that allows religious freedom. But with freedom comes responsibility. You and I have a responsibility to make sure that the religious leaders we listen to, follow the principles in Scripture.

Maybe you're not too concerned about the cults, because you don't see their impact in your neighborhood. But look out! The one thing these spiritually blind guides count on is ignorance. They feed on the sheep that wander mindlessly into their fold.

Don't overreact to cults and false teachers by organizing a witch hunt. But don't fall into the other extreme of ignorance and complacency. God wants you to know the enemy. Don't go through life with a spiritual blindfold on. I'll close with a warning from the Bible.

"Be very careful, then, how you live—not as unwise but as wise" (Ephesians 5:15).

Huddle Discussion

• What do you think it would be like to be blind?
• What is a cult?
• Why should we be concerned with them?
• Have you ever talked to somebody in a cult? What was that experience like? Would you handle that situation any differently today?
• Do you think people are too concerned with cults or are not showing enough concern? Why or why not?
• What is the best defense against the cults?
• Give your advice for the following situation:
Your friend Bob has started to attend the meetings of a new religious group. You think the group might be a cult. What should you do, and what advice should you give Bob?

Just do it!
✔ Memorize: Ephesians 5:15

Fifth spot just fine as KC's Brett sees changing roles

George Brett says he's accepted two things this spring. First, he'll bat fifth in the Royal's lineup. And secondly, he's not "the horse" anymore. Brett who will turn 39 on May 15, thus enters his 20th season with the Royals without the usual heavy burden. He's not expected to carry the club on his shoulders. (Kansas City Star)

No doubt about it. George Brett is one of the greatest to ever play baseball. He helped his team be one of the best teams in their division for almost two decades. He has shown year after year that he has had the right "stuff".

Now his role has changed. He shouldn't feel too bad. After all, nothing stays the same. Now his role on the team will be more supportive. Before, as George goes, so go the Royals, was often true. That probably won't be true in the future. Several of the younger players will carry the team in the future.

When I read this story, I couldn't help but think about another person who had to adjust to a new role. In the Bible, John the Baptist also had to move over and let someone else carry the load.

John had a vital role to play in the world—to announce the coming of the Savior.

He was unique. He lived in the desert, ate honey and locust, and wore camel hair. He was a wild-looking man who had no power or political position in the Jewish community.

Yet, God took this odd man and used him to prepare the way for Jesus Christ. In fact, the response was so great to John's message, that hundreds responded to him.

His role changed. Just as George Brett's role has changed, so too, did John's role on God's team. Eventually, John's loyal followers even became jealous of Jesus. As John's role became less important, more people began to focus on the ministry of Jesus.

John made it clear to his followers that as his role was changing, "He must become greater; I must become less" (John 3:30).

Although I doubt if most of us share much in common with John the Baptist, there is one thing that each of us should share with him. He pointed people to Christ. His mission was to influence others to follow Christ, not himself. Remember, our greatest role in this life is to influence people for Christ, not us.

Huddle Discussion

• Do you think most athletes would have responded to Brett's changing role like he did? Why or why not?

• Who has played a more important role in the success of their teams: Michael Jordan with the Bulls or Magic Johnson with the Lakers. Explain your choice.

• What is the most important position on your team? Why?

• If your coach moved you to a new position that seemed less important, how would you feel? Why?

•Jesus said, "It is more blessed to give than to receive" (Acts 20:35). How does this verse apply to athletics?

• What is more important: To tell others about Christ, or to live out your faith in front of them? Why?

• How can you point others toward Christ, rather than to yourself?

Just do it!
✔ Memorize: John 3:30

SPORTS

Gooden has 'No Fears' after rotator cuff surgery

Dwight Gooden expects to be back in top form next season even though his rotator cuff injury is the one that often puts a pitcher's career in jeopardy. The Met's front office and Gooden were stunned when they were told of the rotator cuff problem. "I'm just happy and satisfied no further surgery will take place," Gooden said. "I have to start exercising, keep the faith and work hard. I don't have any fears. I don't doubt myself." (AP)

Play sports long enough—and you know the type of "fear" that Gooden faces. Sooner or later, most athletes will get hurt. It might be a shoulder, ankle, knee, or whatever. One thing is for sure, injuries are a part of sports.

Not only is there the fear of a possible injury, but like Gooden's shoulder, there can be the fear of reinjury. Finally, the injury every athlete dreads—a career ending injury. Just ask Bo Jackson, or Dave Dravecky.

You don't have to play sports to be fearful. There are a lot of experiences in life that can make us fearful. It could be a test you have to take this week. It might be someone you know who is sick or dying. Fear causes us to become immobilized and intimidated.

God can handle our fears! Listen to what the writer of Psalm 27:1 says, "The Lord is my light and my salvation—whom shall I fear? The Lord is the stronghold of my life—of whom shall I be afraid?"

You see, fear can trap each of us. Whenever we are rejected, sick, hurt, misunderstood, uncertain, or face death, we can become fearful. We can conquer our fears and get rid of the darkness by relying on the light of the Lord who brings salvation.

David, the writer of this Psalm, expressed a lot of confidence in the Lord, when he wrote down these words. And why not? After all, what or who is there that we should really fear, if the Lord is with us? No one! When God provides the light, there is no hole deep and dark enough to keep his light from shining through.

The Lord provides comfort, hope and strength to anyone who is willing to follow Him. Take some advice from the life of Dwight Gooden, "keep the faith and work hard". In other words…go for it.! Stop thinking about your fears and grab on to the Lord. Hold on tight! Lean on His strength. Because he wants you to be confident—no doubt about it—you can count on Him!

Huddle Discussion

• What injury do you most fear? Why?

• What were two fears you had growing up? How about now? What would be the worst thing that could happen if your fears became real?

• When do you most need the Lord's confidence? How does His presence help you deal with fear?

• In what ways is God bigger than fear?

• How does Scripture help you deal with fear?

• What advice would you give to each of these people?

a. Jill just found out she needs knee surgery next week. It's possible that she'll miss basketball season.

b. Pat's dad is an alcoholic and he's not sure if his parents will stay together or break up.

c. Ann and Leslie were hurt badly in a car accident over the weekend. Everyone is worried about their recovery.

d. Bill's brother is dying of cancer.

Just do it!

✔ Memorize: Psalm 27:1

Celtics eagerly await Bird's return Sunday

The Boston Celtics are looking to Larry Bird's expected return Sunday to help them out of their recent tailspin. Bird's impact on the team is more than scoring, reflected in the NBA statistics before his injury, listing him as the league's only player to be among the top 20 in rebounds, assists and scoring average. "He will raise the level of everybody's play up a notch just by being on the floor," said Ed Pinckney, who has stepped into Bird's starting position. (USA Today)

I'm sure everyone looked forward to Larry Bird's return. Well, unless you're a Pistons' fan, you do. Celtics' fans look forward to it because of what will happen when he does return. It's simple: He makes the Celtics a better team when he's in the lineup.

For Christians there should be an eagerness about the return of Jesus Christ. Larry Bird will make a difference when he returns to play basketball, so a much bigger difference will be realized with the return of our Savior, Jesus Christ. If we can get excited about the return of a basketball player, how much more should we be excited about the return of Jesus.

This return is often called the "second coming". Not all Christians understand it. Yet, it's the most important future event that will take place...and maybe soon. A lot of people never give it a second thought. Others think it's a waste of time to focus on the Lord coming back.

I disagree. What's more important than my opinion is that it's biblical to focus on his return. The Bible says we ought to do it in Titus 2:13, "Looking for the blessed hope and the appearing of our great God and Savior, Christ Jesus."

If you read God's Word, you will also find that His return is no minor issue. In fact, one out of every 30 verses in the Bible mentions the return of Christ or the end of time. Only 4 out of 27 New Testament books doesn't mention Christ's return.

Okay, so maybe you agree that it's important to think about His return, but so what? What difference should it make in our lives? A lot of people have misunderstood how to apply this verse to their lives. It doesn't teach us to go out and set dates for his return, or that we should quit school or our job and wait for His return on a rooftop.

It *does* mean we should live every day as if it's our last. Now please don't go out and cancel all your plans for the next few years. Plan like you'll be around for tomorrow, but live your life like he's coming back today.

While Christians might disagree on when He's coming back, one thing's for sure, He will return. Are you ready?

Huddle Discussion

• Do you think most people care about the return of Christ or the end times? Why or why not?
• What would you do differently, if you knew Christ would return at the end of the week?
• A lot of people are concerned with "When will He return?," but the more important question is "Why does He delay His return?" Read 2 Peter 3:9. Discuss how this verse applies to the last question.
• Jesus promised to return for those who believe in Him. But you can't wait and decide what you believe about Him on that day. Do you agree with this statement? Why or Why not? If you agree with this statement, how should it motivate us?
• What is wrong with trying to set dates for His return?

Just do it!
✔ Memorize: Titus 2:13

Don MacLean reaching goals

Imagine being 8 years old and knowing unequivocally what you would be doing with the rest of your life. And being right. Pat MacLean, the mother of UCLA basketball sensation Don MacLean, was looking through a scrapbook recently and discovered an essay her son wrote for his third-grade class. It was titled, "What I want to do when I grow up," and it prophetically said:
- I want to average 27 points a game.
- I want to shoot 87 percent from the line.
- I would like to someday score better than Kareem Abdul-Jabbar.
- I would like to play in the NBA.
- I would like to be in the Hall of Fame. (L.A. Daily News)

He would like to someday score better than Kareem? That's a pretty aggressive goal, isn't it? It became reality a couple of weeks ago. MacLean became UCLA's career-scoring leader, surpassing a 23-year old mark held by Abdul-Jabbar.

Not bad. What about his other goals? He leads the Pacific 10 Conference in free-throw shooting at 91.7 percent and is averaging 20.4 points a game. Most experts think he is a lock for the NBA, and maybe even the Hall of Fame.

Did his goals help him become a better athlete? Listen to what he says, "People can say what they want about me, but no one will ever question my work ethic. Because I have always had goals in mind, many times I've worked harder than my peers."

Goals work. It's really that simple. A goal gives us a target to shoot at. They focus our minds on the task, rather the distractions. Does God care about our goals? Is He interested in what our goals are? Good questions. Let's take a moment to answer them.

God cares about our goals, because he cares about our

work and us. Goals help to determine who we are and what we do. For example: Abraham's goal in the Bible was to follow God anywhere and gather people around him who would walk by faith. As a result, he rescued the Jews and led them toward the promised land.

Although you may set many goals, there is one ultimate goal each of us should strive toward: To glorify God. Here is a verse that lays the foundation for the ultimate goal.

"For you have been bought with a price; therefore glorify God in your body (1 Corinthians 6:20).

Setting goals to win championships, set records, win games is fine. But gloryfing God should be our ultimate goal. What exactly does gloryfing God mean?

We glorify God when we draw attention to Him, not us. We glorify God when we reflect His character and actions. Finally, we glorify God when we cause others to have a good opinion of Him, because of the way we live our lives.

Imagine being 8 years old and knowing unequivocally what God wants you to be doing with the rest of your life. I challenge you: Set goals! Work toward your goals! Make your ultimate goal to glorify God!

Huddle Discussion
• What's the biggest goal you've ever set?
• In what ways have goals helped you?
• How can you know for sure that your goals will glorify God, rather than self?
• Take time to set at least three goals for this season and discuss how you decided on each. Use the following criteria to help determine your goals:
• Will my goals glorify God or are they selfish? (1 Cor. 10:31)
• Did I pray about my goals? (1 John 5:14)
• How will my goals affect me? (1 Cor. 10:23)
• What would Jesus do? (Colossians 3:1)

Just do it!
✔ Memorize: 1 Corinthians 6:20

Dreams vanish in 0.05 of a second

As Julie Parisien readied herself for her second run in Thursday's Slalom, she had visions of Olympic medals dancing in her head. She was in first place after the first run. But, skiing too conservatively, thinking more of finishing than going all out for victory. Parisien finished fourth overall, 0.05 of a second away from a bronze medal. "That was ultimate disappointment," she said of her first look at the scoreboard. "When you realize you basically said, 'Please take the gold medal from me...' That's basically what I did, hand the gold medal away." (USA Today)

Almost every athlete has dreamed of winning a championship, a medal, or something they've put their heart into achieving. More often than not something happens, and suddenly, they know that they will never realize their dream.

Each of us faces different disappointments. One thing is common. It's painful to lose anything we work toward achieving. Most of us put a lot of time and energy into our dreams, don't we? Maybe you've just been cut from the varsity, or made an error that cost you the big game. Maybe you're facing the ultimate disappointment, like Julie Parisien.

So the question becomes, "How do I forget about a disappointment and get on with my life?"

The apostle Paul found the answer and lets us in on it in Philippians 3:13-14, "Brethren, I do not regard myself as having laid hold of it (sinless perfection) yet, but one thing I do: forgetting what lies behind and reaching forward to what lies ahead, I press toward the goal (to be Christlike) for the prize of the upward call of God in Christ Jesus."

It's only normal to let a negative experience influence our

current action. That's why Paul tells us to leave our disappointments completely in the past. You see, Paul's ultimate goal was to be like Christ. There is no way to be 100% like Christ. So, rather than giving up on his goal, he put his mistakes behind him. Then he looks forward to the future.

You can do the same thing when something negative happens to you. Your mind can only focus on 100% of its capacity on one thing at a time. The more you concentrate on letting the Holy Spirit help you be like Christ, the less influence the past disappointment will have on you.

The key is to focus so much on the goal, of becoming like Christ in all you do, that your failures become secondary. If you dream only of records, trophies, and prestige, you'll eventually be disappointed. But if you keep your focus on Christ, forget the past, then look forward to the future, you'll be able to play beyond even the worst disappointments.

Huddle Discussion

• If you could be in the Winter Olympics, which event would you chose? Why?

• What was your most disappointing loss or performance growing up? How did you feel after it?

• What kinds of disappointments have you faced this season?

• Do you think Christian athletes handle disappointment better than non-Christians? Why or why not? Examples?

• Describe how your attitude toward disappointment can affect you and others? How about future competition?

• What helps you deal with disappointment?

• Give your advice for each of the following people:

    a. Bill lost the final race of his career. It also meant his track team lost by a couple of points.

    b. Jill missed the free throw that would have put her team in the state playoff games.

Just do it!
✔ Memorize: Philippians 3:13-14

SPORTS
DEVOTIONS

Pairs: More than sum of its parts

Figure skating is usually regarded as a highly individual sport. One athlete, one pair of skates, one rink. But it takes partnership, cooperation and understanding to succeed in pairs skating. I talked with some skaters who have competed in the Olympics about their experiences as part of a pairs team. They agreed one of the keys is that as one half of a pair, you must worry about you and your partner at the same time—unlike a singles event in which you're concerned only about yourself. The bottom line about pairs skating might have been said best by former Olympic skater, Sandra Bezic. She said pairs skating is like joining two puddles of water. You link them, let them fill in and form one balanced pool. (USA Today)

The article goes on to explain that one of the most important factors for a pairs team is to learn to read each other, to communicate on the ice. In other words, to work together as a team. Pairs skating is all about teamwork.

Teamwork is not just important to pairs skating. Almost any sport involves teamwork. It's putting together the different individual talents and blending them, so they can accomplish more than they could on their own.

A team that works together can accomplish much more than the separate members working individually. That's what is called "synergy". The word synergy means that "the sum total is greater than the total of the separate parts." There have even been some scientists who believe if you could get all the muscles in your body to pull in one direction, you could lift over twenty-five tons.

It shouldn't surprise us to find out that God has a lot to say about teamwork. After all, even the Trinity: God, Jesus, and the Holy Spirit are a blend of three different parts—that become more than the sum of its parts.

One of my favorite verses on teamwork is Ecclesiastes 4:9, "Two are better than one because they have a good return for their labor."

This verse teaches that it makes sense to work together—we can accomplish more as a team, than by ourselves. We need to trust others and be a team member. It's better to have someone along side in life, than to go it alone.

In 1 Corinthians, it says, "you are a temple of the Holy Spirit." The word "you" is plural. In other words, together we are the temple of the Holy Spirit. Together we glorify God.

It doesn't matter what sport you play, teamwork doesn't work, unless you help to make it work. We all need to relate and respond to each other. You see, someone needs you, and you need someone.

You don't have to be a skater to understand that teamwork is like joining two puddles of water. Each of us needs to do our part to link up with others and form one balanced pool.

Huddle Discussion

• When you were growing up, which team did you most enjoy playing on? Why?
• What happens when one part of the team makes a mistake?
• Which sports team do you think best represents teamwork? Why?
• What are some examples of teamwork in the Bible?
• What are qualities that every team needs to work together successfully?
• In what ways do we bring glory to God as a team?
• In what ways have you seen teamwork work?
• Buckminister Fuller, in his book *Synergetics*, explains that it is possible that "one plus one can equal four if we put our efforts together in the same direction." In what ways can this be true of your team?

Just do it!
✔ Memorize: Ecclesiastes 4:9

Bob Knight can't shake reputation

Bob Knight once said his goal was to outlive his enemies. That might be the only way the Indiana basketball coach will shake a reputation built as much on controversy as success. Forget the three NCAA championships, the 10 Big Ten titles, the Olympic and Pan Am golds, his near-600 victories and selection to basketball's Hall of Fame. The image Knight has created, and almost seems to relish, is one of a man who screams at officials, throws chairs, berates the media and battles his own temper. (AP)

He's been called the "classic bully" by other coaches. Some have called him the ultimate bad boy of basketball. And yet, I can't help but feel that there is more to this coach, than we sometimes read about in the sports pages.

Knight's antics seem to overshadow the honesty and loyalty he expects from himself and his players. He doesn't make promises to player, he doesn't keep. And former player, Steve Alford, once said he kicked three players off the team for smoking marijuana, dismissed another for cutting classes, and benched four starters, including Alford, because he said they hadn't been working hard enough.

Here is a coach that hates cheating and follows the rules as closely as possible. Yet, if you were to ask people on the street their opinion of him, it might reflect more the negative stuff than the positive.

I believe your reputation is who people think you are, and that your character is actually who you are. Who you are when nobody is looking, is really who you are—that's your true character. I think we as Christians need to also be concerned with our reputation. I know God is more concerned with character. But a damaged reputation can only hinder your witness for Jesus Christ. For sure, nobody is perfect. On the other hand, nobody wants to listen to someone they don't respect.

The handbook on wisdom puts it this way, "A good name is more desirable than great riches; to be esteemed is better than silver or gold" (Proverbs 22:1).

The idea in this passage is that an honorable reputation because of good character, is much more valuable than having a lot of wealth. Nothing we can obtain or accomplish is more important. Not even a silver or gold medal.

In sports, it doesn't take much to damage a reputation. A slip of the tongue, or a temper that goes unchecked can easily happen—and often does. Once the damage is done, it's difficult to rebuild your reputation. A good reputation, built on solid character is important. What good is a reputation if it is built on controversy, rather than godly success?

Huddle Discussion

• List the top five athletes you most respect. Why did you pick these particular athletes?

• List the top five coaches you most respect? Why did you pick these particular coaches?

• How does character affect your reputation?

• If you could choose what your reputation would be with others, what kind of reputation would you pick? Why?

• In the book of Proverbs, it says that someone who betrays another person's confidence will never lose a bad reputation (Proverbs 25:9, 10). Why is it so difficult to shake a bad reputation?

• How do you respond to someone you don't respect?

• What is the result of a Christian who has a bad reputation?

• What can you do to guard your reputation?

Just do it!

✔ Memorize: Proverbs 22:1

Griffey talks about suicide

Ken Griffey Jr. just wanted to be a normal teen-ager. With an emphasis on *normal*. The son of an All-Star ballplayer and himself on a fast track to stardom. There were times he felt the price, the sacrifices, were too great. One time in particular, in January 1988, fed up with a lifestyle too focused to enjoy life, the 18-year old Griffey swallowed a couple of hundred aspirin tablets. Griffey, now just 22 and the heart of the Seattle Mariners, went public with his story in Sunday's *Seattle Times,* hoping to dissuade others from seeing suicide as a solution. "Don't ever try to commit suicide," he said. "I am living proof how stupid it is." (USA Today)

What happened to Ken Griffey Jr. is becoming more common in our society. It doesn't just affect athletes—but millions of teen-agers who are trying to deal with life.

Listen to what Griffey told a reporter about how he felt just before he tried to commit suicide, "It seemed like everyone was yelling at me in baseball, then I came home and everyone was yelling at me there. I got depressed and angry. I was really mad at myself more than anything."

Griffey who often speaks to school groups, hopes his story will help others realize how widespread the problem is among athletes. "Who would have thought Magic Johnson would have the AIDS virus?" he asked. "Who would have thought Ken Griffey Jr. would attempt suicide?"

Athletes often feel like they are placed in a fishbowl for everyone to watch. If you fail—everyone sees you lose. If you make a mistake—everyone sees it. While athletes put pressure on themselves, sometimes parents, friends, and family add to it.

Sometimes the pressure to perform closes in like a vise.

Athletes often don't see anyway to get away from the pressure that is making life seem unbearable.

There is a Greek motto that says:

You will break the bow if you keep it always bent.

It might be time for you to loosen the strings before the bow breaks. For some, it's already too late. Each day in the United States, over seventy people commit suicide.

I've found one particular Bible verse that has helped me overcome worry and frustration: "Trust in the Lord with all your heart, and do not lean on your own understanding. In all your ways acknowledge Him, and He will make your paths straight" (Proverbs 3:5-6).

It's important to understand from this verse that you need to respond to the pressure by trusting God. In other words, it's your choice—nobody can do it for you.

When you feel pressure build—take time to reflect on Proverbs 3:5-6. Then, totally trust God, not relying on your own perspective, and depend on Him for your strength and direction. I'm convinced that God wants you to be living proof how smart it is to commit your life to follow and trust Him. The solution to all our problems is Jesus Christ.

Huddle Discussion

• When have you felt the most pressure in sports?
• How did that pressure make you feel? How did it affect your performance?
• What are some other areas of your life where you feel stressed out? Why?
• Whom do you feel the most pressure from: Friends, family or coaches/teachers? Why?
• How do you try to get rid of stress?
• Do you think suicide is a big problem? Why?
• What do you think makes life worth living?
• If a friend said, "I wish I were dead!" what would you do?

Just do it!

✔ Memorize: Proverbs 3:5-6

Magic Johnson tests positive

Magic Johnson, whose beaming smile and sparkling play entertained basketball fans for more than a decade, announced Thursday that he had tested positive for the AIDS virus and was retiring. "Because of the HIV virus I have attained, I will have to announce my retirement from the Lakers today," Johnson told reporters gathered at the Forum, where he played 12 seasons with the Los Angeles Lakers. (AP)

Of all the sports headlines in this book—this was the biggest in 1992, maybe the decade. I can't think of anybody who wasn't stunned by the news. I can remember hearing the news and thinking, "No way—it can't be true!"

I waited for months before I sat down to write this devotional. Even now I have a lot of mixed feelings about what happened to Magic. After all, he was one of my heroes, too. I've still have a painting on my office wall of him that I've had up for more than a decade.

I don't want to crucify Magic, nor do I want to make him a hero for getting the AIDS virus. There is nothing heroic about getting AIDS. In fact, I'm not sure coming forward with the news about contracting the virus was heroic, either. There wasn't really anything else he could have done.

I was concerned about his initial message, which focused primarily on using condoms, so that you could have "safe sex." The idea was that what happened to him could happen to anyone who didn't use condoms.

Give Magic credit. Once he realized his message was

unbalanced, he announced that no sex was the safest sex.

Relying on condoms for "safe sex," is a little bit like putting on your seat belt just before you drive recklessly into a dangerous curve. Yes—it's safer, but it's a lot safer to drive carefully.

No, I'm not ready to take down Magic's picture on my wall. In fact, I'm more convinced than ever that he needs people like you and me praying for him. It's only through a relationship with Jesus Christ that he can beat AIDS. He still may lose his life here on earth, but he can still chose to spend eternity with Jesus.

I'm sure Magic is a sport's idol. That's a no-brainer. But it's not the same thing as hero. A hero does something heroic or courageous. Magic has shown a lot of guts on the basketball court over the years, but now he really has a chance to be a hero. It all depends on what choices he makes in the future.

I hope you realize that AIDS can affect all of us—but only if we let it. It might sound old fashioned—it is. But the safest protection from AIDS is what many people wear on their finger—a wedding ring. It's more than just wearing it—it's sticking with the commitment that goes with the ring.

Huddle Discussion

• How did you feel when you heard the news about Magic?
• If you were in Magic's shoes, what would you do differently, if anything? What would your message be now?
• Do you think the news about Magic had any affect on the way people live their lives? Why or why not?
• Do you think AIDS is a judgment from God?
• How should we as Christians respond to people who have the HIV virus?
• Read Mark 1:41-42. How did Christ treat the lepers differently from how we treat outcasts of our day?
• If a friend said, "I have the HIV virus", what would you do?

Just do it!
✔ Memorize: 1 Corinthians 13:1

Cunningham gets buddies to help

Call it Camp Cunningham. Philadelphia Eagles quarterback Randall Cunningham, coming back after missing most of the 1991 NFL season because of knee surgery, is paying the expenses to fly four of his favorite receivers to Las Vegas for a week of workouts. Cunningham has spent more than $30,000 for air fare, expenses, equipment, and rental of the field, office space and gymnasium, said his business manager Terry Bender. I've never heard of anybody doing something like this before," said one of the receivers. (AP)

What a great way to get back into shape. Cunningham's sessions included film study, conditioning and passing drills. Eagles coach Rich Kotite called it "a good way to prepare, mentally and physically." I agree.

What will help make his recovery plan work is the support from his buddies. There is nothing like having friends to support and encourage us, when we most need it. I have a feeling that Cunningham's $30,000 investment will pay dividends far beyond what anybody can imagine.

Even if we're not trying to make a comeback—we need other people. It says in the Bible that, "Two are better than one because they have a good return for their labor. For if either of them falls, the one will lift up his companion. But woe to the one who falls when there is not another to lift him up" (Ecclesiastes 4:9-10).

True friendships are needed but rarely happen on their own. An interesting verse in the Bible on friendships is found in Proverbs 18:24. "A man of many friends comes to ruin, but there is a friend who sticks closer than a brother." The word *ruin* literally means "to be shaken so violently that you fall to pieces."

In other words, the Bible is teaching that we need a few close friends that we can count on. If we can't find those friends, we won't have the support we need. Many friendships are broad, but not deep. We all need to build friendships that have depth to them.

How do you build this type of friendship?

First, be open to the other person. It's impossible to develop a solid friendship, without being open and honest about yourself and others.

Second, develop an attitude of acceptance. We all need to feel loved and accepted. No friendship can survive without this kind of attitude.

Now let me ask you: Do you have friendships that are based on openness and acceptance? If not, it's time to start. I doubt if you can afford $30,000 to fly your buddies to be with you, when you need them. I know you can start to develop friendships that are supportive. This week…yes, this week, when you get together with your teammates to work out, start to develop friendships that are based on honesty and acceptance. Call it Camp Jesus.

Huddle Discussion
- How do most people chose their friends?
- What qualities do you look for in a friendship?
- How have your friends stuck to you closer than a brother?
- What does it mean to be open and honest with your friends? How about accepting? Give examples.
- Proverbs 27:5-7 says, "Better is open rebuke than love that is concealed. Faithful are the wounds of a friend." How does this verse apply to friendships? Give some examples.
- It's been said, "If you want good friends, you need to be a good friend." What does this mean?

Just do it!
✔ Memorize: Proverbs 18:24

McCartney's views spark controversy

A University of Colorado coach who became a hero for turning around a losing football team is getting jeered for using his title and popularity to preach evangelical Christian views against homosexuality. McCartney, 51, revived a Colorado football program in 1982 and led the team to the national championship in 1990. Outside work, he said, he feels mandated to take a stand on homosexuality. "I may be a football coach, but I'm not going to stand aside on the tough issues facing society," he said. (AP)

This article raises several important questions. First, is homosexuality a sin? Second, should a Christian take a stand for moral values in our society, regardless of the pressure put on them personally? Third, should a particular lifestyle receive certain protections from society? Fourth, if you oppose homosexuality, are you a "hate monger" or "self-anointed ayatollah," as one politician accused McCartney of being?

There isn't enough time in this devotion for me to discuss each of these important questions. I'll try to touch briefly on the first question and leave the last three for your group discussion.

There was a time in our society when nobody wanted to talk about homosexuality. Now you can't miss the moral battles on TV. If it's not a dispute over some piece of art being funded by the National Endowment of the Arts, it's a protest in New York by gay people who want to be included in the St. Patrick's Day march.

Is homosexuality a sin? There are several places in the Old Testament where homosexuality is condemned as sin.

Leviticus 18:22 says, "Do not lie with a man as one lies with a woman; that is detestable."

It's true that Jesus didn't specifically talk about this sin. It just wasn't a problem among the Jews. The apostle Paul did talk about it because it was a common problem in the Greco-Roman culture he ministered to. Although, Jesus didn't speak about homosexuality, he did talk about human sexuality. Whenever he spoke on an issue like divorce, it was assumed he was coming from a heterosexual position, he always pointed back to the Creation for the basis of his arguments.

The apostle Paul gives us the most specific verse in the New Testament on homosexuality. In Romans 1:26,27 Paul condemns the actions of both lesbians and male homosexuals. He said that both men and women exchanged their natural relations for unnatural ones.

Many churches today even accept and promote homosexuals into leadership roles. Society should not set the standards for Christians. Just because homosexuals have considerable political clout, doesn't mean Christians should adopt their set of standards.

We need to remind ourselves that as Christians, we have a responsibility to take a stand for moral issues today, but we also need to recognize that God is willing to accept anyone who is willing to come to him in faith. We need to love the sinner and hate the sin.

Huddle Discussion

• Do you agree or disagree that homosexuality is a sin?
• Should a Christian take a stand for moral issues, like Coach McCartney did? Why or why not?
• Should gays receive special rights?
• If you oppose the homosexual lifestyle are you a "hate monger" or "self-anointed ayatollah?" Why or why not?
• What can Christians do to help homosexuals?

Just do it!
✔ Memorize: Leviticus 18:22

Knight's bullwhip merits complaints

About 150 calls complaining about a photograph showing Indiana coach Bob Knight flipping a bullwhip toward the rear end of bent-over black player Calbert Cheaney, have been received by the NAACP. "The phone has been ringing off the hook," Alice Hoppes, president of the Albuquerque chapter of the National Association for the Advancement of Colored People, said Friday. "I've heard from people who said they thought it was an outrage." Indiana's sports information director said Knight was joking at the time. (AP)

Was it a joke? Maybe, but if it was a joke a lot people didn't get it. Regardless of Knight's intent, a lot of people, especially black people, are not happy about the message a photograph like this sends to others.

Some people in America think bigotry and racism have been overcome. Knight's action with the young black player just goes to show the insensitivity of one race toward another.

I'm not trying to judge whether or not he is a racist or bigot. In fact, I doubt if he is. Knight has worked hard to help many of the black athletes that have played for him. Maybe what bothers me the most about what he did is that this attitude is more common than any of us want to admit. Most white people don't run around wearing white robes and burning crosses. But many white people might tell a joke, and not even realize how it makes someone of another race feel.

In sports, there seems to always be somebody talking or writing about the differences between the races. A popular movie, *White Men Can't Jump*, is an example of what a lot of people believe about blacks and whites in sports.

The Bible has a lot to say about how God looks at the differences between races. His perspective has never changed. "God does not show favoritism" (Romans 2:11).

Some of us have seen firsthand the problems with the hatred of bigotry and racism. Most of us have seen insensitivity and lack of understanding between the races. In fact, I doubt if any of us are totally without some prejudices. I think the cure for these problems is that each of us respond in obedience to God's Word. We need to love one another, just as Jesus did.

Jesus met a Samaritan woman at a well and loved her enough to change her life. Some of you, I'm sure know the story. Maybe what you've missed is how he overlooked the fact that she was from a race of people that he shouldn't even have talked to—much less helped. But he did.

It takes understanding, love, concern and a heart to do what God would do to overcome problems between races. As Christians, we need to do more than just give lip service to changing the way people treat each other. Each of us has a responsibility to speak out when favoritism or unfairness is shown, because of race. And that's no joke.

Huddle Discussion
• Define the following terms: racism, bigotry, and prejudice.
• Are blacks better athletes? Why or why not? How are these stereotypes negative?
• How prejudiced are you on a scale of 1 to 10? Why?
• Have you ever been affected by any of these terms?
• Where have you seen these attitudes at work or school?
• What affect have they had on you and others?
• Do you think interracial dating and marriage is wrong? Why or why not?
• What steps can be taken to overcome race problems where you live?

Just do it!
✔ Memorize: Romans 2:11

For would-be dunker, only block is mental

Seven years ago, West Virginia's Georgeann Wells became the only woman to dunk in a women's college basketball game. A 6-foot freshman could change all that. North Carolina forward Charlotte Smith, niece of former NBA player David Thompson, has the physical skills to pull off the feat. It's her mind that gets in the way. "I've had two fast breaks this year, but I chickened out," said Smith. "Getting up and holding on to the ball isn't a problem. I can get up there. I guess I worry so much about missing—that's my problem." (USA Today)

Mental blocks stare all athletes in the face. It doesn't matter if you run track or play golf. Sooner or later, something will appear impossible. After all, take the four minute mile. At one time, it was thought to be a barrier that was unbreakable. For example, look at the long jump. When Bob Beamon set the world record, many so-called experts predicted that his record would never be broken. They said it just couldn't be done. But it was broken, wasn't it?

Do you have any mental blocks? Maybe, you don't see how you can possibly break into the starting lineup. Maybe you don't think you can jump higher, run faster or throw farther.

Almost anything can become a mental block. And they aren't always found in sports. Some students think they can't achieve higher grades or get into college.

In the Bible, the greatest example of a man who refused to let anything or anyone be a barrier, was Noah. You remember the story from Sunday School. Here was a man that God told to build a huge ark and fill it with two of every kind of animal. You can bet there were a lot of people who tried to tell him to stop. He refused to let anything get in his way of serving God.

Noah did what many thought was impossible. When Bob Beamon broke the world record, it seemed he had accomplished the impossible. When Roger Bannister broke the four-minute-mile barrier, it seemed like a miracle. Yet, each of these feats probably had more to with removing the mental blocks, than anything else.

Listen to what God says about removing barriers, "Because you have so little faith, I tell you the truth, if you have faith as small as a mustard seed, you can say to this mountain, 'Move from there to there' and it will move. Nothing will be impossible for you" (Matthew 17:20).

Now don't miss the point here. Jesus didn't mean this verse should be taken physically and literally. After all, most people don't need to remove a physical mountain. He meant that if you have enough faith, all problems or barriers can be solved, and even the hardest task can be accomplished.

I don't know if God wants you to break a world record— or even the school record. I do know that he wants you to compete without mental blocks. As Yogi Berra might say, "Mental blocks only get in your way."

Get rid of the mental blocks in your life. Start to depend on God for what seems impossible or improbable. Just maybe, you'll be surprised by how much He can do through you!

Huddle Discussion

• What is your mountain or mental block in sports? Why?
• Are there any barriers or blocks in the rest of your life? If so, what are they? Why do they exist? What can you do about them? Do you believe that God can remove your problem?
• In what areas can you begin to apply a little more faith this week?

Just do it!
✔ Memorize: Matthew 17:20

Teenage confidential

Jennifer Capriati has something to say. Get out of her room. Also, get out of her life. Do you understand? Here's what happens when a girl turns 16 years of age, as Jennifer will this Sunday. She shoots poisonous looks at her mother, who shakes her fist and says between clenched teeth, "I can't wait till you have kids!" She answers every question with an impudent "So?" If you really want to send our Miss Capriati into a rage, call her current state of mind a phase. More accurately, it's a rite of passage that virtually every adult has experienced: teenage rebellion. " Her hormones are kicking in," says her mother. (Sports Illustrated)

Tennis star, Jennifer Capriati, isn't going through anything that most teens don't experience—except that she is one of the best tennis players in the world. Who wouldn't be tired, confused and sulky? Really, it's all part of growing up, isn't it?

Most teens want to be independent from their parents. They want their own identity, to be their own person, and to make their own choices. Parents often view this attitude as rebellion. Teens see it as healthy and absolutely necessary.

About the same time, the hormones kick in. It makes a confusing mess! Nobody is happy. Nobody is satisfied with the situation. Yet, life must go on.

How should parents and teens deal with this problem? The advice from the talk shows is shallow and empty. Advice from friends is seldom constructive. God has given us the answers in the Bible—for both parents and teens.

Parents do have a responsibility to treat their children with respect. Sometimes that doesn't happen. It doesn't take the kids off the hook from obeying their parents.

Remember, God has commanded children to obey their

parents, even when they seem to be wrong. The first of the Ten Commandments that attaches a promise to a commandment says, "Honor your father and your mother, so that you may live long in the land the Lord your God is giving you." (Exodus 20:12).

What does it mean to honor your parents? It means speaking positively about them and politely to them. It means to show them courtesy and respect. To not obey them, is to disobey God.

Believe it or not, most parents want the best for their children. They have invested a lot in them. They are usually concerned about their future.

Parents may not be perfect, but they are the only parents most of us will ever have. God gave us parents and we need to be thankful for them. The Ten Commandments are not suggestions.

Most teens may experience the rite of passage of teenage rebellion. Every teen can choose to move beyond it. The teen years need not be a battle ground between parents and teens. Don't rationalize and say, "Well that's just the way I am." Call it what it is—rebellion. And say, "Lord, I need your help." Only He can turn turmoil into understanding. Only He can smooth the rough waters that develop between teens and parents. Take my advice: Turn to the Lord. Do it now. You'll be glad you did sooner, than later.

Huddle Discussion
• What is the most fun you've ever had with your parents?
• What are two things you like about your parents?
• What are two problem areas with them?
• Are you getting closer to your parents or farther apart? Explain your answer.
• How can God mend relationships between parents and teens?

Just do it!
✔ Memorize: Exodus 20:12

Horace Grant Converts

Horace Grant, Chicago Bulls forward, underwent some personal changes. "My wife and I were having a lot of problems," I admitted. And a lot of it was my fault. I wasn't treating people right, especially my wife." So with her help, Grant began a conversion to Christianity. "I was sliding spiritually," Grant said. "I knew I had to do something, so I personally gave myself to the Lord. I realized He gave me so much, but I wasn't really giving back to Him all that I should. For Grant that meant staying home. He quit the local nightclub scene populated by several of his teammates and began staying in his room on the road, reading the Bible. (Omaha World-Herald)

This sports headline is an excerpt from the book *The Jordan Rules.* While there was quite a bit of controversy about the book, I found this particular part of it interesting.

What is conversion? For Horace Grant it meant a change in behavior. He had to admit he had done something wrong, then turn to the Lord for help. For him, it meant changing some of his old habits. It meant changing the way he treated other people. It meant reading a Bible, rather than reading the bar menu at nightclubs.

To "convert" means to change from one form to another. We talk about many types of conversions in sports. In football, we convert extra points and field goals. In basketball, we convert turnovers. Some teams and players find it easy to convert opportunities into success.

People are difficult to convert. True conversion comes only by God's help. We can't convert anyone! Only God can through the Holy Spirit. He uses the Holy Spirit to change our hearts, so that we repent and are converted.

This was the game plan the Apostle Paul preached, he

said, "Repent, then, and turn to God, so that your sins may be wiped out" (Acts 3:19).

John the Baptist prepared the way for Jesus by preaching a message of repentance. In the Gospels, Jesus called conversion "repenting of sin" or "entering a narrow gate."

So then, what must each of us do to be converted? Is it really possible for anyone to be converted? Does it matter what type of person we are? Is there hope for anyone?

Yes, there is hope only in Jesus Christ. There is only one requirement for entering the Kingdom of Heaven: Jesus said, "You must be born again."

Have you been converted to Christianity? Have you been converted to a personal relationship with Jesus Christ, or have you simply "got religion." For Horace Grant it meant turning away from his sin, and inviting Jesus Christ to have a personal relationship with him as Lord and Savior.

If you feel like you're sliding spiritually—stop! Give yourself to the Lord the way Grant did. You can be sure, you can know without a doubt, that you are part of God's eternal team in the Kingdom of Heaven.

Huddle Discussion

• What is the most impressive sports conversion you've seen?
• Can you relate to Horace Grant's conversion? Why or why not?
• Repentance means to turn away from our former way of life. It's a spiritual U-turn. How was this true in Horace Grant's life? Can you relate to this in your own life?
• The Bible teaches in 2 Corinthians 5:20 that conversion makes a person a "new creation." What do you think this verse means? What sort of changes should take place when someone becomes a Christian?
• What do you think is the difference between "getting religion" or "being converted to Christianity?"

Just do it!
✔ Memorize: Acts 3:19

USA can't bend the rules for O'Brien

Dan O'Brien still is the best decathlete on the face of the earth, but he's not going to Barcelona, a circumstance that might make some wonder about the way the U.S. chooses its Olympic track team. O'Brien failed to clear his opening height in the pole vault,, 15-9, a standard he regularly makes in practice and a height lower than he cleared in warmups. He went from flirting with a world record to zero points in the event at the U.S. Olympic Track and Field Trials Saturday. And zero chance of making the Olympic team. Occasionally, there's the appearance of a grave injustice being committed, and someone suggests a waiver system for those people. Once you start cutting breaks, where do you stop? (USA)

I had just finished cutting the grass and had flipped on the TV to see that Dan O'Brien was not in first place in the decathlon. In fact, he wasn't even in the top four places. I couldn't believe it! I thought maybe NBC had added up the scores wrong.

Bruce Jenner, former decathlon champion, called O'Brien's failed attempt a "tragedy" and most people agreed. Especially—Reebok! They had invested 25 million dollars in a Dan vs. Dave ad campaign that was shot down before the end of the day.

No, the Dan vs. Dave issue won't be settled in Barcelona. It does bring up another issue that athletes are confronted with—rule bending. O'Brien himself, I'm sure, isn't looking for a bye or any favors. It's tempting to confuse sympathy with fairness. There is no such thing, as a sure thing. Just ask former Olympic competitors Jim Ryun or Mary Slaney.

Spiritually speaking, one of the most misunderstood issues when trying to understand God is mercy vs. justice. "How can a loving God send people to Hell?" For many people, it doesn't make sense. Just as it seems like somebody should bend the rules for Dan, why shouldn't God bend the rules for those who are headed to Hell?

First, He didn't make us robots. Each of us have been given the ability to choose right or wrong. He gave us the ability to choose to love and worship Him. But the first humans chose against God and doomed their descendants to do the same unless God stepped in to save them.

Because God is just, the only way to save man was to pay the penalty for the sin man had committed. So, God sent Jesus Christ to suffer and die to pay the penalty for our sin. "For God so loved the world that he gave his one and only Son, that whoever believes in him shall not perish but have eternal life" (John 3:16).

God loved us enough to send His Son to die for us. This is how He shows His love toward us. He is also a God of justice. He can't or won't bend the rules that He established.

Although there is no rule bending, when it comes to God's judgment, he does give us a chance to choose eternity with or without Him. That's fair. The only tragedy is when some chose not to believe in Him. God's only waiver system is for those who believe in His Son—Jesus Christ!

Huddle Discussion

• What is the most unfair situation you can remember in sports? Why do you feel that way?
• Do you agree with God's system of mercy vs. justice? Why or why not?
• Read John 14:6. Why is Jesus the only way to salvation? Why can't we bend the rules, so there would be other ways to heaven?
• How does God show His love and mercy toward us?
• In what ways did God make man different from other creatures?

Just do it!
✔ Memorize: John 3:16

Red's Dibble trying to control his temper

Like the rest of America, Cincinnati Reds reliever Rob Dibble paused last summer to consider the behavior of one Rob Dibble. This lightning rod of a relief pitcher came to a very reasonable conclusion: Sometimes, Rob Dibble can be a colossal pain. He has been described as thoughtful and introspective as well as hotheaded and a "a little baby" by Reds owner Marge Schott. He has been fined or suspended six times over the last three seasons. Dibble has a rap sheet of temper tantrums that dates back to his earliest days with the Reds. In spring training 1989, he took a bat to patio furniture and tossed a few chairs into a lake—after giving up a home run in an exhibition game. (St. Petersburg Times)

The "Rules of Living," suggest how we should deal with anger: When angry, count to ten before you speak; if very angry, a hundred."

Later, Mark Twain, modified it to: "When angry, count four. When very angry, swear."

The Red's Dibble has probably tried both philosophies and struck out. If most of us are honest—we haven't done so well ourselves. A bad temper can lose games, lose friends, and hurt our families. Anger needs to be talked about, understood, admitted, and kept under wraps, or it will damage much more than how we perform in sports.

Let's examine a key verse in Scripture on how to control anger in Ephesians 4:26,27, "Be angry, and yet do not let the sun go down on your anger, and do not give the devil an opportunity."

At first glance, it looks like God is saying, "Get mad!" And that's true, but don't miss what God is trying to teach in this verse:

First, when is it right to get mad? Consider the behavior

of Jesus Christ. Jesus himself showed anger when he drove the money changers out of the temple. He later, nailed the religious teachers to the wall with his words. The only time in Scripture where anger is okay is when God's Word or will are disobeyed. It's not okay to blow up for the wrong reasons or when things don't go our way.

Second, anger is an emotion, like love, that God has given you and me. There is nothing unusual about expressing either emotion. It is not necessarily any worse to get angry, than to show love. It's at the point where anger becomes sin, that it becomes wrong.

Third, in this verse Paul gives us two things to watch carefully when we start to become angry. He warns us not to stay angry. When we do, don't give the devil an opportunity to use our anger to serve his purposes, rather than God's.

Few of us have a rap sheet as long as Dibble's. We're all made differently. Some are very emotional, like Dibble. Some wouldn't show emotion if they won an Olympic medal! That's part of how God put us together. Each of us needs to control our anger. We can either chose to control our temper with God's help, or we can chose to let it control us. Either way, the choice is yours.

Huddle Discussion
• What situations make you the most angry in sports? Why?
• Why is it difficult to keep from losing our cool?
• Read Proverbs 22:24,25. How can this verse help you deal with anger?
• Proverbs 15:1 says, "A gentle answer turns away wrath, but a harsh word stirs up anger." How can this verse be applied to your athletics? Other areas of your life?
• James 1:19 says, "But let everyone be quick to hear, slow to speak and slow to anger." How can you apply this verse?

Just do it!
✔ Memorize: Ephesians 4:26,27

Lemieux: Graves' blow intentional

Mario Lemieux broke his silence and accused Adam Graves of the New York Rangers of intentionally hurting him in the second round of the Stanley Cup playoffs. "It was intentional, no question about it," the Pittsburgh center said as he prepared for the third game of the Stanley Cup finals on Saturday night against the Chicago Blackhawks. "I've never been hit that hard in my life." Lemieux's left hand was broken when Graves slashed him early in the second game of the Patrick Division finals. (AP)

Watching Graves' slash Lemieux during an ESPN report, I could almost feel the pain. The blow was savage. It sidelined the best player in the NHL and reinforced the already poor image hockey has for unnecessary violence.

While this incident brings up the issue of violence in sports, it also brings up another issue most of us are faced with in competition. What to do when somebody hurts us or takes unfair advantage of us. In basketball, it might be elbow to the head or face. In baseball, it might be a pitch that is thrown into the batter's head.

So what do you do when someone nails you? I'll never forget a friend of mine telling me about an NFL linebacker who was challenged with following the example of Christ in sports. He just couldn't figure out how it could be done. He complained about how the centers in the NFL often took cheap shots at him during the games. So, my friend asked him, "Randy, what do you think Jesus would do in your situation?" The linebacker stood up, smacked his hands together, and said, "I think he would kill him!"

While most of us realize his response is not what Jesus taught or lived, many of us have struck back when someone tried to take advantage of us. The Bible is very clear on how we should respond when someone has hurt or injured us in some way.

"Let all bitterness and wrath and anger and clamor and slander be put away from you, along with malice. And be kind to one another, tender-hearted, forgiving each other, just as God in Christ also has forgiven you" (Ephesians 4:31-32)

That's it! For a Christian, there is no keeping score or getting revenge for an act against us.

Here is the best way I know to sum up forgiveness. First, think about how much God has forgiven you. Focus on the mercy He has had on you. Never forget how He has canceled your debts against Him. Second, confront the resentment or bitterness you have toward the person who has wronged you. It's important to forgive and then forget. Don't hang on to your bitterness or anger. Put it in the past. Ask God for the strength to forgive and forget.

No question about it. God not only loves and forgives you, He demands that we follow His example. Pray. Ask God for his strength. Choose to forgive and forget the offense. Do it now.

Huddle Discussion

• What is the most violent act you've seen in sports? Why do you think it took place?
• How can you find the balance between being a push-over or being someone who strikes back out of anger and resentment, when wronged?
• How can you forgive and forget? Read 1 Cor. 13:5, Matt. 7:1-5, Ps. 119:165).
• From the life of Christ, what are some ways he handled unfairness?

Just do it!
✔ Memorize: Ephesians 4:31-32

Pastor: Howe mixed with wrong people

Steve Howe's pastor believes the "Lord's intervention" led to the pitcher's arrest for cocaine possession last week. "There's no denying from Steve of being involved with people he shouldn't have been involved with," said Al Barone, pastor of the Valley View Foursquare Church in Whitefish. The 33-year-old Howe, who made a comeback last season after a 3 1/2 year absence from the major leagues, was arrested Thursday and charged with possessing cocaine. Howe has been suspended from baseball five times because of drug or alcohol problems. (AP)

I can't help but root for a guy who is working hard to make a comeback—especially when he confesses to be a Christian. But it's hard to swallow Howe's failure when he has already been suspended from baseball five times.

Anybody who has played sports has got to be confused. Here is a guy who is making great money, playing a game he loves, yet can't stay away from drugs. It seemed like Howe was in a safe place in remote Wyoming. After all, wasn't this a place far away from the temptations of drugs?

His pastor said something that was at least part of his problem—mixing with the world. Jesus told his disciples in John 17, that they were to be "in" the world (vs. 11), but not "of" the world (vs. 16).

This is one of the most important verses in the Bible. It teaches that since we live in the world, we are involved with the world. How involved should we be? The New Testament clearly teaches that we need to be careful to not become entangled with it—like Howe did.

When Jesus said his disciples were to be "in" the world,

he meant they mixed with people who were their neighbors, but who may oppose God's system of values. They might live next door or be your teammate, but they may not share the same set of values.

When Jesus told his disciples not to be "of" this world, he meant they were not to get their values from the world. Instead, they were to their get values from God's system.

While it's okay to mix with the world, it's not okay to get them mixed up. In other words, we are not to mingle with the world, but rather we are to witness to the world. Like Christ, we are to love the people in the world, but not their sins.

Here is where the rub lies: to associate with and love those in the world without being influenced or swayed by them. We need to keep from being contaminated by their values. We should be in the world, but the world should not be in us. It's okay for the ship to be in the sea, but it's bad when the sea gets into the ship.

Simply put, the Bible says, "Do not conform any longer to the pattern of this world, but be transformed by the renewing of your mind" (Romans 12:2). It's not just refusing to conform to certain behaviors and customs. It's also letting the Holy Spirit redirect our minds.

In the final analysis, chose to follow God's set of values— *your choice*. There is no neutral ground when it comes to values. Don't mix your worlds up, or you may find yourself suspended from God's values.

Huddle Discussion

• "To be a Christian we can't dress or act like the world?" Do you agree with this statement? Why or why not?
• How can you love the sinner, but not the sin?
• How can you keep from allowing yourself to be contaminated by the world?
• How can the Christian athlete be "in" but not "of" the world of competitive athletics?

Just do it!
✔ Memorize: Romans 12:2

Promiscuity risky business for athletes

The pickup usually happens soon after a game, outside the locker room or in a hotel lobby by women chasing more than a player's autograph. "They come up to you, catch you for your autograph and then ask if you're single," says Robb Dibble, pitcher for the Cincinnati Reds. "Girls want to touch you. They put you on a pedestal. It's out there if you want it." The post-game scenario is as much a part of the ritual as *The Star-Spangled Banner.* There's little romance in the matchups. After a National League baseball game several years ago, a reporter watched a prominent player emerge from the clubhouse and walk over to five women waiting outside. After carefully studying each, he chose one with a nod and left with her. (USA)

The lifestyle of many athletes, pro or otherwise, can be risky business. Many place themselves in positions to become targets of sexual temptations. For them, the temptations are just too much. If you question the risk, ask Magic Johnson.

For some athletes, the role of playboy or athlete is one-in-the-same. Wilt Chamberlin boasted of sleeping with thousands of women during his playing days. The playing around has little to do with romance for either partner.

The problem is lust. It's not a new problem. In the Bible, one of the strongest men, Samson, was dropped in his tracks by lust. Lust was the one enemy he couldn't beat. He was attracted to the opposite sex by outward appearance *only*, not unlike many athletes today. Samson, when lusting after a woman said, "Get her for me, for she looks good to me." A lot of athletes say or think that same thing about the opposite sex.

Lust is a problem because it affects everyone. It's impossible in our society to avoid the junk that pours into our homes through TV, movies, and music. These three areas of entertainment alone, put many wrong desires in front of our eyes on a regular schedule.

So what's the solution? Unplug the TV? Boycott the movies? Burn the records? No, though, we could all probably do without some of the things we watch or listen to. If you try to resist temptation on your own—forget it. Many have tried and failed. There is only one way to beat lust.

"No temptation has seized you except what is common to man. And God is faithful; he will not let you be tempted beyond what you can bear. But when you are tempted, he will also provide a way out so that you can stand up under it" (1 Corinthians 10:13).

Let's get specific.

First, you haven't seen or heard anything new. Wrong desires or temptations happen to everyone. Second, others have beaten lust or temptations, so can you. Third, follow the Bible's advice on beating temptation. Here's how: (1) Identify the people or situations that give you problems. (2) Get away from anything you know is wrong. (3) Decide to do what is right. (4) Pray for God's help and support yourself with friends who will help you resist temptation.

Don't mess with lust. The first look might be harmless. But eventually, you'll get burned. After all, you don't have to be an athlete for promiscuity to be risky business.

Huddle Discussion

• Why are people attracted to athletes?
• Why do you think many athletes fail to resist lust?
• Genesis 39 records the story of a man who resisted temptation by running away from it. How can this work in someone's life today?
• Which form of entertainment do you think provides the most wrong desires or temptations for you? Why?
• Discuss each of the four steps for beating temptation.

Just do it!

✔ Memorize: 1 Corinthians 10:13

Tom Osborne takes a stand

It's third-and-1. Coach Tom Osborne is going deep. What better way to describe Osborne's decision to go for it when asked to have his image on 20 billboards in Omaha and Council Bluffs decrying pornography. "I'm in a position where some people might value what I have to say," Osborne said. "One time I heard Burt Reynolds on TV—and I'm certainly no Burt Reynolds—but he said he regretted that he had some opportunities to make a difference in some things and didn't do it. If it helps two or three kids somewhere, makes one father or some guy think a little bit before he gets involved with pornography, it will be worth it." (Omaha-World Herald)

Good call coach! But Coach Osborne is not alone in this drive to stamp out pornography. More and more athletes and coaches are speaking out in the fight against pornography.

Anthony Munoz, one of the NFL's best offensive lineman, refused to have his picture taken by *Playboy* magazine, when he was named to the All-American team. Later, in his pro career, *Playboy* called back to do a feature article on him as part of it's preseason football issue. Again—Munoz, turned them down. For more than two years, he has been a part of Cincinnati's Citizens Concerned for Community Values.

Pornography is big business, estimates range as high as $10 billion per year. Some estimates show that there are four times as many adult bookstores in the United States as there are McDonald's restaurants. And cable TV and "dial-a-porn" telephone services have made it even more accessible. While children and women are exploited in the name of free speech, the impact on those who use the pornography is impossible to measure.

Researchers may argue over the amount of influence

pornography has on people, but one thing is clear. It does influence our behavior. If advertisers spend millions of dollars each year to influence our behavior to buy their goods, isn't it obvious that the images people see in pornographic magazines would leave their mark?

The Bible says, "For as a man thinks within himself, so he is" (Proverbs 23:7). The idea is we become what we think about. We're influenced by the images we put in our mind. Just ask Nike. They've built a shoe empire on adds based on the images of Michael and Bo.

So what can you do to take a stand against pornography? First, stay away from it. 1 Corinthians 6:18 says, "Flee from sexual immorality. All other sins a man commits are outside his own body, but he who sins sexually sins against his own body."

Second, speak out against it, when given an opportunity. No game is won by one person. And pornography is a problem that needs the help of all of us.

Whether you're an athlete or not, it's likely that people value what you have to say. Don't be shy! Make the call. You can make a difference, but only if you take a stand.

Huddle Discussion

• Why are people attracted to pornography?
• What are the negative effects of pornography?
• In what ways is "garbage in, garbage out" true of pornography?
• Do you think pornography can be addictive? Why or why not? What can someone do that thinks they are addicted?
• The Apostle Paul says, "Be very careful how you live—not as unwise but as wise, making the most of every opportunity , because the days are evil" (Ephesians 5:15, 16). How can you apply this verse to the issue of pornography?

Just do it!
✔ Memorize: 1 Corinthians 6:18

Wrestlers' singular quest: gold

The USA's wrestlers are on a mission. Ask them what they're thinking about. Gold medals, they'll answer. To them, it's not trite, not some Olympic gush and gloss. Some, those who've never been there, admit they repeatedly picture themselves getting the gold. They call it motivation, mental preparation. They visualize the big match— it's tied with 10 seconds to go. And then, in their mind they make the winning move. (USA)

Motivation.

It may be the single most important part of athletic performance. Either you have it, or you don't. No amount of ability can compensate for a lack of it. Either you're on a mission to win, or you're not.

For the Christian athlete, motivation comes from a different source than simply getting a medal. While other athletes might be motivated by accomplishment, greed, selfishness, recognition, or a host of other things, a Christian athlete should be motivated by one thing: service to God.

Dave Johnson, an Olympic Silver medalist in Barcelona, has found this new motivation in Christ. Listen to how his motivation is different than most. "There's no limit to what Christ can do in my life. Through getting to know him, I have found new purpose. I want to study his Word and grow in my knowledge of him. God calls me to do my best, so I give 100% of myself for him. Then, when I have done my very best, I leave the results entirely to him. Even if I take last place, I rejoice in the fact that I gave everything I had and accept the result as part of his plan."

A lot of the things that motivate us can let us down. Think about it. If revenge motivates you to play your best—what happens when you aren't playing a team that you don't have a grudge against? What if you're motivated by recognition—but your team is in last place. Maybe, you've noticed how some pro athletes play their best the year before they become a free agent. Once their financial future is secure their intensity drops. Yes, greed or financial reward may motivate some athletes, but it's not consistent.

What motivates Dave Johnson *does* work consistently. It doesn't depend on circumstances. In other words, you don't need to be playing your rival to get up for the game. And It doesn't matter how far ahead you are in the match, you'll still want to play your best.

Paul gives us the reason we're to be motivated to serve God in Romans 12:1. "Therefore, I urge you, brothers, in view of God's mercy, to offer your bodies as living sacrifices, holy and pleasing to God—which is your spiritual act of worship."

Paul is teaching us that by thinking about God's mercy toward us, we will become motivated to play our best for Him. It's a way we can serve and worship Him. Church isn't the only place we go to worship God. We can do it on the court!

Want to get mentally prepared for your competition? Visualize what Jesus has done for you on the cross—then do your best to please Him. It's the only way to make the winning move from God's perspective.

Huddle Discussion
• When were you motivated to play your best? Why?
• Define motivation. What is the difference between the way Dave Johnson is motivated and others?
• What are the problems with the way some motivate themselves to win? (Greed, recognition, money, etc.)

Just do it!
✔ Memorize: Romans 12:1